Your Green Career

The handbook for young women and
non-binary changemakers

TRACI LEWIS

Published in 2023 by Discover Your Bounce Publishing

www.discoveryourbouncepublishing.com

ISBN: 978-1-914428-18-0

Page design and typesetting by
Discover Your Bounce Publishing

"Traci's insights into the journey of young women and non-binary changemakers as they begin their green careers are invaluable. Her ability to inspire and empower will have far-reaching impacts as the young people she connects with lead the charge in creating a safe and viable future for us all." **Amelia Twine, founder of Sustainable Fashion Week**

"A brilliantly written, essential read for young women wanting to make a difference!" **Natalie Fee, author, campaigner, founder of City to Sea**

"This is a fantastic handbook for any young female activist. The Catalyse Change programme really supported my changemaker journey." **Mya-Rose Craig (Birdgirl), author, youth climate activist**

"Traci's barrier flattening, irrepressible enthusiasm, and determination trumped my old, straight male logical resistance at every encounter. Twenty years of tearing up the rule book and not accepting no as an answer makes her the living embodiment of the need for and power of diversity in all its forms. If anyone can lead us to redemption it might just be Traci." **Guy Singh-Watson, founder of Riverford Organic Farmers**

"Everybody needs a community to support them to change the world, and I think this programme provides that backbone very well. Thank you so much for encouraging diverse and underrepresented people to come forward and help save the planet." **Yasmeen, Catalyse Change alum**

CONTENTS

"I am convinced that climate change represents a historic opportunity on an even greater scale."

Naomi Klein, activist, author

"Every job has the potential to become 'green' as the world moves to combat climate change, and there are a huge range of skills which will support the transition to a net zero economy."

Green Jobs Taskforce

This book is based on learning from Catalyse Change's sustainability empowerment and green careers programme. Catalyse Change CIC is a social enterprise that inspires and upskills young women and non-binary changemakers. All profits from sales of this book go to the further development and delivery of this programme.

www.catalysechange.com

www.instagram.com/catalysechange/

Three key terms explained:

What do we mean by a 'green career'?

Green Careers have a direct, positive impact on the climate and are focused on sustainability. We define this as working in roles and/or for organisations whose core objectives are to provide environmental protection or social justice. Green or climate jobs are essential to our future low-carbon economy.

However, there isn't currently one universally accepted definition of green jobs or careers, and often, the term is only used to refer to those with an environmental focus.

The United Nations defines sustainability as: "Meeting the needs of the present without compromising the ability of future generations to meet their own needs." It has three pillars: environmental, social, and economic.

You cannot solve the climate crisis without social justice, so we use the term 'green career' to mean both. We will explore these issues further throughout this book.

What do climate and social justice really mean?

Climate justice is a movement and practice that recognises that the climate crisis is a social and political problem, as well as an environmental one. It acknowledges that different communities feel the impacts in different ways and that the responsibility for the crisis rests with some countries and companies more than others.

It recognises the disproportionate impacts of climate change on low-income and BIPOC (Black, Indigenous, People of Colour) communities around the world, the people and places least responsible for the problem. The aim of climate justice is to do everything possible to stop global warming from increasing those inequalities.

Social justice is a movement that believes in the equal distribution of wealth, opportunities and privileges within society. Some of these movements focus on particular aspects of this, for instance racial and gender injustice.

What is the difference between equality & equity?

Equality suggests that everyone is at a particular starting point and should be treated the same.

However this can only work if everyone starts from the same place and needs the same level of support.

Equity recognises that each person has different circumstances and allocates the exact resources and opportunities needed to reach an equal one. It aims to give everyone what they need to be successful.

SECTION 1:

SETTING THE SCENE

How this book will help you

Do you ever feel anxious, scared, or overwhelmed in the face of the climate crisis?
You want to help but need to figure out how you can effectively do something about it.
Do you need some inspiration and guidance about how you can make a difference?

If you want to be a changemaker, it's quite a time to be alive. We are at a time of critical transformation and need everyone to help. This book will help you understand how you can be part of it. To help grow your confidence, develop your skills, and know you can make a difference.

The good news is that anyone can work in sustainability. You don't need to be a scientist or have loads of technical skills or experience.

What you do need is to believe that you can do something about society's biggest challenges.

At Catalyse Change, we have developed a programme to help you create the mindset and learn the skills to do this. I will help you explore how you can be part of the solution by sharing tools and tips from our Catalyst Programme.

I'm also writing this for my younger self. The book I wish I could have read when I was feeling lost. When I knew I wanted to make a difference in the world but didn't know how.

So many clever, generous, and wise people have guided me. So, here I will share some of the learning and wisdom that helped me on my changemaker journey.

I hope this book will:

- inspire and help you to move quickly and decisively
- provide reassurance when you're struggling
- equip you with tools and ideas for your next steps
- help you on the next leg of your incredible journey.

However, it's your journey, and it's OK to do it in your own time, at a pace that works for you. I look forward to sharing this part of it with you. Thanks for reading.

"The best time to plant a tree was 20 years ago. The second best time is now." **Chinese Proverb**

Why girls and women?

Our life support systems are under immediate threat.

We are at a critical time in our human and planetary history.

It is time for transformative change. To move away from the capitalist model, to use our resources responsibly, and create a circular economy that provides equal benefits for everyone.

"So, we are left with a stark choice: allow climate disruption to change everything about our world, or change pretty much everything about our economy to avoid that fate. But we need to be very clear: because of our decades of collective denial, no gradual, incremental options are now available to us."

Naomi Klein, author & activist

Girls and women comprise over half of the world's population. We must be empowered and skilled to help create structural changes and other solutions for survival.

However, the system is stacked against us in so many ways. Patriarchy is alive and kicking, and the structural power in our social, political, and economic systems is weighted in men's favour.

Yet countries and governments such as Finland and New Zealand, when led by women – Sanna Marin and Jacinda Adern – have implemented impressive environmental and social policies for the well-being and survival of our people and planet.

Women leaders were better at leading countries during the global Covid-19 pandemic from 2020 to 2022. One study found that outcomes related to Covid-19, including the number of cases and deaths, were systematically better in countries led by women. Female-based principles of collaboration, communication, and empathy appear to provide a better approach when dealing with social and ecological emergencies.

- Research suggests that firms with greater gender diversity in their management reduce their carbon dioxide emissions by about 5 percent more than firms with predominantly male managers.

- Banks with more women on their boards tend to direct more significant finance shares toward sustainable investments.
- Countries with a higher representation of women in their parliaments are more likely to ratify international environment treaties.

Women face a particular set of challenges:

- **Gender pay gap**: this was still 14.9 percent in the UK in 2022 – down from nearly 20 percent five years ago – but is still too much, considering money equals power in our society.
- **Senior leadership**: in an IBM study women held only 18 percent of senior leadership positions among 2,300 organisations surveyed worldwide. In other words, men occupy approximately 82 percent of the most influential roles in today's organisations.
- **Confidence gap:** women often feel less confident in their abilities or are perceived negatively in the workplace when they display confidence. Social conditioning and unconscious bias play a huge role

in this.

Why non-binary people?

We are inclusive of all women, non-binary and gender non-conforming changemakers. As gender identity is a highly personal part of who we are and how we perceive and express ourselves. This book includes people who do not describe themselves or their genders as fitting into the category of either man or woman. Non-binary is used here as an umbrella term for people whose gender is not entirely and exclusively male or female. It is a broad definition as non-binary means different things to different people. So where women are mentioned in this book please take it to mean non-binary too.

How do we change it?

Change must occur throughout society to stop perpetuating and reinforcing gender stereotypes and unconscious bias.

To help provide solutions, Catalyse Change CIC – the social enterprise I co-founded in 2016 – inspires, empowers, and up-skills young women and non-binary people as sustainability leaders and changemakers.

We created the Catalyst Bootcamp and online Catalyst Summit – a sustainability empowerment and green careers programme – followed by six months of mentoring with a woman working in sustainability. I have written this book to share some of the learning from this programme.

Catalyse Change's three programme pillars are: personal development and well-being, green education and careers, and sustainability knowledge and green skills. Using a holistic approach, we create an environment that supports you to be 'the change you wish to see in the world'.

We believe achieving a low-carbon, sustainable future requires a transformation in thinking, with equity and sustainability at its core. The active voices of young women and non-binary people – who bring different perspectives and ideas for change – are vital for achieving this.

What are we trying to address?

- **The UK has yet to achieve gender equality in**

employment or leadership. We are one of the world's richest countries, but failing our girls. We are failing to meet international standards set out in human rights frameworks.

- **Women remain typically underrepresented in STEM** (science, technology, engineering, or mathematics jobs). Stereotypes, negative perceptions, and poor understanding of career options hold girls back.

- **The challenges facing young women diminish their confidence and resilience**. These include cyberbullying, body image, anxiety, and other mental health issues.

- **Advice on education and career options in the sustainability sector is limited**. Many schools need more support to enable young people to pursue the extensive and rapidly evolving range of career opportunities now available.

Women are most affected globally

I'm a white woman in the UK, so I am writing this from a position of privilege. By this I mean that I have unfair societal advantages because of my skin colour, background and where I live.

The groups most vulnerable to the impacts of our climate crisis are those least responsible for its causes. Climate change already disproportionately affects people in the Global South – a problem they have done little, if anything, to create. Africa is responsible for the smallest share of global emissions, at just 3.8 percent, compared to China and the USA, with a combined share of 40 percent. Yet Africa faces devastation from floods, droughts, and famine due to rising sea levels.

Climate justice demands that everyone is treated equally and fairly, especially those who have done the least to cause it but who are experiencing its worst effects.

Women and girls globally are the group most vulnerable to the impact of climate change, with Black and Indigenous women being even more exposed. They are often more at risk and yet are powerful agents of change, both in reality and perception.

Climate justice and gender equity need to be achieved because a sustainable future depends on it.

"Climate change is a man-made problem that requires a feminist solution." **Mary Robinson, politician, 7th President of Ireland.**

It's a feminist issue

- Feminism is the belief that women and all genders are entitled to political, economic, and social equality.

- Feminism is committed to ensuring women and all genders enjoy their rights on an equal footing with men.

- Intersectional feminism is the idea that all of the reasons someone might be discriminated against, including race, gender, sexual orientation, gender identity, economic class, and disability, overlap and intersect.

My green career

One of the first women I truly admired – other than pop stars like Debbie Harry, Annie Lennox, and Madonna – was Anita Roddick. In the 1980s, she was a rock star to me.

She was a businessperson, activist, and campaigner who founded the Body Shop – the chain of body care shops that pioneered ethical consumerism. They told compelling stories about the products and the people who made them, with memorable campaigns highlighting animal cruelty and social injustice.

This was the first social enterprise I had ever heard of, and I loved it. It fired up my passion for activism, equality, and how social business can be a vehicle to help create a better world.

However, my top priority then was to go and explore the world. As soon as my A-Levels were finished, I worked until I could afford a round-the-world plane ticket and I was off. I left behind my sleepy Warwickshire village – where my dad, sister, and I were born – to have adventures.

It was in Australia that I started to become more

environmentally aware. I lived in the desert, sapphire mining and watermelon picking, and worked as a short-order cook and hotel room cleaner on two tropical islands.

- These places had no fresh drinking water. It was either shipped in or sucked up from ancient aquifers, a non-renewable source thousands of years old.

- In SE Asia, I saw rivers clogged with plastic and whole mountains demolished to build high-rise apartments, as well as visible gender and social discrimination.

- I experienced air pollution so thick that you couldn't see more than a few feet ahead. They were wearing masks in Asia long before the coronavirus pandemic.

This all helped me understand what sustainability meant and why it was so important.

Discovering Permaculture

I studied Permaculture design in Australia with its founder Bill Mollison to help me understand and find solutions for sustainability. Permaculture is a philosophy and design system that mimics nature to find the most sustainable ways of living. Organic food production is critical, but it goes much further than that; from demonstrating authentic, sustainable living, to the power of community networks and also the importance of our inner journey.

To learn more, I spent a few years – between paying jobs – living and working on organic and biodynamic farms. Also, getting free bed and board while continuing my travel odyssey. It made me realise that the university place waiting for me at Swansea wasn't for me. Anyway, in the early 1990s in the UK, I would have spent more of my time raving than studying. Much better to be exploring new parts of the world, experiencing a new way of looking at and understanding myself and the world.

Also, this is where I found my purpose. I realised I wanted a career in organic food and farming as it provides hugely positive solutions to the massive problems facing our people and planet.

So, when I returned to the UK and happily discovered my beloved Bristol, I asked the Soil Association based there for a job. It was 1997 and I started working for their social business.

Over the next 18 years, I had a fantastic career with them, which taught me so much and enabled me to live in Cornwall and Devon as manager of their regional office Organic South West.

However, I knew I really wanted to start my own social enterprise before it was too late. Although I had many excellent skills and contacts, I was a single parent and lacked capital. Also, I wasn't sure exactly what I wanted to create. It was 2014 and I was living in beautiful Totnes in Devon but had received a strong intuitive steer to return to Bristol, which I was considering...

Message from an oak tree

Then, out of the blue, I found myself talking to an oak tree! Bear with me...

I had just been to a mystical shamanic healing retreat in Devon for my birthday, which had affected me deeply. The final message I received from the shaman was to ask an oak tree how I could give back to the world. Really, how could I refuse?

So, this is how I found myself receiving a life-changing piece of wisdom from a beautiful, ancient oak tree. The tree told me I needed to help empower young women. I didn't know how, but it came from a deep inner knowing, and I knew it wasn't something I could ignore.

Empowering girls and young women

So, I began to inform myself about the important issues and support women's charities. When I moved back to Bristol, I became a trustee of Integrate UK – a youth-led charity – campaigning on gender rights and social justice issues.

However, my interest and networks were all about sustainability. I realised that Catalyse Change – for which I'd already registered the company and domain name – needed to focus on empowering girls and young women as change agents for sustainable development.

I had already been talking to women in my networks and was delighted when three brilliant women, Jenna, Julie, and Rhian, said yes to helping me make the dream a reality.

We changed Catalyse Change to a CIC

(community interest company) and began to develop a vision and plan for what we would create. We've now worked with thousands of young women and have had some transformational results. Yet we are still only at the start of our journey. I'm excited and full of hope for what we can achieve. The possibilities are limitless. Would you like to join us?

I know it's easy to laugh at things we don't understand – it's a natural reaction – but don't underestimate the power of trusting your intuition. And if you pass an oak tree one day, why not sit down and chat? Who knows where it might lead.

Why now? Why you?

We are in a climate emergency. Everyone needs to get involved and provide solutions.

> *"If not now, then when – if not you, then who?"*
> ### Hillel, a first-century Jewish scholar

We have until 2030 to halve our current greenhouse gas emissions, to stand a chance of stabilising our global climate change to 1.5C and achieving net zero[1] by 2050.

We also require social justice – to stop the enormous global inequalities created by the capitalist system – which is responsible for this climate crisis.

But did you know we already have the knowledge and skills required to achieve net zero?

Project Drawdown, a leading resource for climate solutions, has demonstrated that not only can we stop global warming but also reverse it, by reaching a point

---

[1] Net zero refers to a state in which the greenhouse gases going into the atmosphere are balanced by removal out of the atmosphere. The term net zero is important because, for CO_2 at least, this is the state at which global warming stops.

of starting to 'drawdown' carbon out of the atmosphere. Drawdown is when atmospheric greenhouse gas concentrations stop climbing and decline steadily, thereby preventing future climate change.

From electricity generation to education, food to forests – all systems can help capture more carbon than they generate.

There are many solutions out there; most have been around for years. Yet we get side-tracked thinking we can only solve it with new technology and innovation. While crucial climate tipping points risk being passed the longer we continue to stall. However, our success is now down to political will and the social and behavioural changes required to implement the solutions.

"I used to think the top environmental problems were biodiversity loss, ecosystem collapse, and climate change. I thought that with 30 years of good science, we could address these problems, but I was wrong. The top environmental problems are selfishness, greed, and apathy; to deal with those, we need a spiritual and cultural transformation. And we

scientists don't know how to do that."

Gus Speth, environmental lawyer

With political will and public buy-in, profound behaviour changes are possible. The Covid-19 pandemic showed us this; social distancing, mask-wearing, and people paid by the Government to not go to work. It also demonstrated the power of collaboration when we all work together.

An inner and outer journey

The speed and level of change that is now required, mean we must go much deeper than just cutting carbon.

To avoid planetary and ecological catastrophes, we need a shift in consciousness.

As Einstein famously said: "You can't solve problems using the same thinking we used when we created them."

We have created political and economic structures that are no longer fit for purpose.

We need to change our mindset to create the ones we need now.

This is why Catalyse Change focuses as much on the inner journey as the outer. It is why we work with young women who already know they want to make a difference.

Change needs to happen quickly and we know women can create such powerful change. We see this time and time again when women lead; Caroline Lucas, Greta Thunberg, and Christiana Figueres, to name just a few. Will your name be on that list too, someday?

However, you don't need to be an activist or politician to make an impact. We all know amazing women who are already making a massive difference at all levels of society, but we still need equal representation where critical decisions are being made. At the 2021 UN climate summit COP26, women numbered 34 percent on committees, and 39 percent led delegations, despite the UNFCCC Gender Action Plan requiring 50 percent participation of women in all levels of climate action.

"Only a quarter of the world's parliamentarians are women. They are just underrepresented absolutely everywhere... That is

what we're calling for, 50:50 vision. That means co-leadership between men and women. Because you wouldn't sail the world with one eye firmly patched up if the waters are choppy, why would you hold international climate negotiations with women missing? It just doesn't make any sense."

Bianca Pitt, co-founder, She Changes Climate

Women's empowerment

Women's empowerment can be defined as our ability to determine our choices, promote our self-worth, and our right to influence social change. In the Cambridge dictionary, to empower means 'the process of gaining freedom and power to do what you want or to control what happens to you.'

Girls and women still face significant challenges worldwide. They receive unequal pay for equal work and face barriers that affect their opportunities. They still need to be represented equally in positions of power and decision-making roles.

To help address this, the UN Global Compact and UN Women have collaborated to create seven women's empowerment principles, which include equality, respect, well-being, and education, to help women thrive in their workplaces and communities. Female empowerment represents the awareness, both individually and collectively, that women can be owners of their actions and lead their own lives.

This book will explore how we can empower ourselves and each other through various activities, from; education and awareness-raising to building our self-confidence, collaboration, and community building.

"There is no limit to what we as women can accomplish."
Michelle Obama, US attorney, and former first lady

My aim for this book is to help equip you with the confidence, inspiration, and tools to 'be the change you wish to see in the world.' To do this, we will cover:

Section 1: Setting the scene: Provides the context for this book and how it will help you.

Section 2: Finding your path: Helps you explore tools for developing your inner world.

Section 3: Becoming a changemaker: The pathways and skills needed for your green career.

Section 4: Building your community: To help you find people and networks to support you.

Section 5: Choosing your future: Final inspiration and ideas for your journey.

ALWAYS REMEMBER – YOU ARE ALREADY THE CHANGE.

You are an amazing and unique person. No one is exactly like you, and there will never be another you again. It is not a coincidence that you are here or reading this book. You were born at a crucial moment in our human history. You are already a changemaker and an essential part of the story of our planet. What role will you play? This book is here to help you decide.

Seven tips for making the most of this book

1. **Use a journal.** Treat yourself to a lovely new journal to help capture your ideas and reflections. It will improve the quality of your learning, and you can revisit it later. Or use your phone or computer if you prefer. There are some excellent apps to help, e.g., Evernote and OneNote. However, there is something special about writing by hand in a journal which enhances the quality of your connection, creativity, and reflection.

2. **Do the exercises**. At the end of each section, three to five practical activities will help you explore the ideas more thoroughly. If you prefer to read the whole book first, it is OK to go back and do them later. However, please do them; it will make your experience and learning from this book more successful. You can use the spaces underneath the exercises to record your initial reflections and actions. Your journal can then complement this.

3. **Write notes**. If you have a printed version, use it to make notes in the margin and underline anything you want to remember or come back to quickly. This is your guided journal – use it any way that works for you. So, grab a highlighter, Post-its, or just a pen – physically interacting with the book will help you to remember and learn more effectively.

4. **Practice gratitude**. Gratitude helps increase your happiness, self-esteem, and positivity. I invite you to perform a daily gratitude practice. Write in your journal, every morning and evening, three things you are grateful for (make them as specific as possible). If you want to ramp up the benefits, try an hourly gratitude practice – or when you remember throughout the day – for a week and see how you feel.

5. **Find community**. We are in a critical situation now. Understandably, you might feel worried or scared. So, seek support from like-minded friends and communities through online and local groups,

clubs etc. Also, join our Catalyst Summit, masterclasses, and meet-ups.

6. **Set intentions**. Intentions are purposeful, powerful tools that can guide you throughout your day. Each morning ask yourself how you want to feel today, what role you want to succeed in, and how you want to affect others. It is about using your mind to frame and direct your expectations and desires. **Try this out in your new journal.** *What is your intention for this book? What do you want to experience and learn?*

7. **Use the resources.** There is a list of valuable books and online sources at the back of this book to help you develop your knowledge, networks, and skills.

SECTION 2:

GETTING STARTED: FINDING YOUR PATH

Finding your path

Everything you see and do in the world reflects what is happening in your mind. To begin your changemaker journey, you must first focus on observing and transforming your inner world. What are your beliefs about yourself? How are they affecting your life experience? Here are some key ideas and tools to help you explore this.

"Create the highest, grandest vision possible for your life, because you become what you believe." **Oprah Winfrey, American talk show host, television producer, author**

Build the foundations

When you set up a new business, you explore and articulate your purpose, vision, and mission.

It helps you understand what you are doing and why. A 'north star' to guide your passage.

So that is what we will do here first, to help guide your green career journey.

When you reflect on your motivations, strengths, and gaps, you are better informed about what tools you need to help you achieve personal and professional growth.

However, you cannot rush this; we will return to it throughout the book, so don't worry if you haven't cracked it by the end of this chapter!

Find your purpose

It seems we are constantly being urged to *'find our purpose'*. But what is it, and how do you do it?

I like Simon Sinek's (author of *Begin With Why*) approach: "What is your why? Why are you doing this? What is it that makes your heart sing? Or what motivates you?"

He says people aren't bothered about what and how you do something. They are interested in the underlying purpose and passion behind it. He cites Apple as a company that has successfully articulated and communicated its WHY, going on to build a world-leading business, brand, and community around it. Here are a few tips to help you find yours:

1. Consider what moves you deep inside.
2. What makes you emotional, angry, and passionate at a deep, visceral level?
3. What makes you want to get out of bed in the morning?
4. What do you care about? What makes you come alive?
5. What makes you want to get on the streets and

shout about it?

6. What issue would cause you to write to your MP?

What is my purpose?

Gender equality is something I feel passionately about. I care about equality, full stop. But gender equality and equity has fired me up since I was young.

I am angry about how women have been treated and marginalised throughout history. Even harder to bear is that this is still happening worldwide, including on my doorstep here in the UK.

Around when I turned 40, I received a strong calling to help empower girls and young women, leading me to set up Catalyse Change CIC. Although I felt this calling from a young age, it was years before I could fully articulate and act on it.

It has involved enormous effort and commitment. I changed my career, set up a business, and built a new network of collaborators. I had to maintain faith in my ability to do it, even when it seemed impossible.

It has been a challenging option, especially when I see friends my age with large salaries, own homes and secure jobs. At times, I do question what I'm doing.

It can make me doubt myself when I compare myself to others like that. Yet I have an incredibly abundant life – I always have what I need and more – which is an essential lesson in itself.

Following your purpose will help you to attract the people and resources you need to achieve it.

People, events, and other opportunities will begin to appear when you decide and start to act toward fulfilling your purpose. These events are not coincidences; they happen when you set your intentions and deliver actions around what you believe in. When you take the first steps, e.g., join an environmental group, write a blog, or help at a local food bank, you will meet others who can support you.

That is why having a purpose is so important. Purpose can drive you when you think it might be easier to give up and get a 'normal job' instead. It keeps you focused and motivated.

When you know your purpose – much like when you know you are in love – you feel it deeply and must just go with it.

But don't worry if you are not in a position to do it yet, everyone has different circumstances, and you must follow the right path for you, right now.

However, whatever your current situation, exploring what drives you is still a good idea. Here are a few ideas to help:

Ikigai philosophy

Ikigai is a Japanese philosophy for a happy, healthy life. It roughly translates as your '*reason for being*' or what makes you *'jump out of bed in the morning.'*

It's the place where your needs, desires, ambitions, and satisfaction meet. A place of balance.

It represents the intersection of four key areas:

- What you are good at
- What do you love doing
- What the world needs
- What you can generate an income from.

At Catalyse Change, we find it is an effective tool for helping you find your purpose.

To find your Ikigai, you'll need to generate a list of things that apply to you in each of the four areas. You then try to find the points where they intersect.

To get started on this, try out the exercises on page 45. We will explore the other two areas later on.

Create a vision for your future

A vision is also a powerful tool for helping you imagine how you want the world to be. To create a vision for your life and the world you want to be a part of.

Businesses and organisations always use a vision statement to outline their future goals and aspirations.

Why not create your own to help guide and inspire your changemaker journey?

My strong sense of purpose makes it easier to articulate my vision:

A world where women (including me) are sustainability leaders and confident changemakers, equal and free, living our best lives.

Creative visualisation

Creative visualisation is a specific way of using your imagination. It's a cognitive process that consists of forming vivid mental images. Try using it to practise visualising the future you want to create.

Try these steps:

- Imagine as clearly and realistically as possible what you want to happen.
- Do it as if it has already occurred or is already happening.
- Thus, creating an inner experience of what it would be like to have your desire come true.

The process is so simple that you can do it at any moment. Just close your eyes – or open is fine if you prefer – and imagine your desired goal as if it is already true. You can make it part of your natural way of living and thinking at any moment.

Imagining the future you want

Radical Imagination is also a powerful tool. Where we collectively envision the world how it could be. It is about recognising that the world should change and that we can do something about it.

In Tori Tsui's excellent book, *It's Not Just You*, she says, 'Radical imagination is an opportunity to envisage the world, its inhabitants and structures, beyond what they are currently. It is a practice of forging realities rather than escaping them. It's an invitation to imagine what could be if anything were possible.'

A great book and podcast that also explores this is, *From What If to What Next* by Rob Hopkins.

He says that these positive visions of the future have great power, 'one of the things all great movements have in common – those that have brought about real change like the Civil Rights movements, the Suffragettes, and LGBT rights campaigners – is that the campaigners have been able to create and sustain a vision of the world they want, tell stories about it, and bring forward leaders who can make that vision a collective one, such that it becomes a powerful narrative – and a powerful counter-narrative to cynicism and despair.'

Mission: how will you do it?

Once you can articulate your world vision, you can work on how you will achieve that – which becomes your mission.

A good mission statement is usually a two to three-sentence summary of why and how you do something and the value you bring.

Our mission at Catalyse Change is to empower, inspire, and skill young women and non-binary changemakers by providing the knowledge, connections, and networks for them to pursue purpose-led careers.

There is plenty of time for action – more on that soon – however, laying the strong foundations for your purpose, vision, and mission will put you in a better position to act effectively.

Values: what gets you out of bed in the morning?

Values are at the core of who we are. They are the behaviours we prize above all others. Ones that give our life meaning and against which we judge ourselves and others.

When we live according to our values, we do more than just talk about them; we practise them too.

The amazing Brené Brown – a researcher, storyteller, and Texan – describes it as:

"We walk our talk – we are clear about what we believe and hold important, and we take care that our intentions, words, thoughts, and behaviours align with those beliefs."

We can learn much from Brené, so check out her books and Ted Talks. She examines human connections based on her research and insights into courage, vulnerability, shame, empathy, and leadership. To help you uncover your values, try out her exercise below.

In summary

- **WHY**: Purpose guides you. Your purpose is why you do what you do, why you exist, and why you serve a higher purpose (your cause).

- **WHAT**: Vision is where you aspire to be. What you will achieve in the future, the measurable impact you will have, and the difference you want to make.

- **HOW**: Mission drives you. It is how you will accomplish your purpose; what guides you every day. It's a direct path to your goals and vision.

Try out these exercises to help you explore yours…

Exercises

1. **Create a vision board:** To help you bring your dreams to life, create a vision board for your life and career. *What is it that you want? How do you want to feel? How do you want your life to improve? What change do you want to make?* You can do this the old-fashioned way using magazines, scissors, and glue. Get a sheet of cardboard and draw a big circle divided into six segments, each representing the most critical areas of your life, e.g., **Friends & Family - Love & Relationships - Travel & Adventures - Work & Success - Money & Abundance - Health & Well-being**. Then find and stick pictures that inspire you in the appropriate sections. Notice the predominant images, colours, moods, and where your desires overlap between areas. You will then have an exciting and valuable visual record that you can keep. I do a new one at the beginning of each year, however, I now use Pinterest instead of paper. The Padlet website (https://padlet.com/) also provides a good tool.

2. **Visualise your dream life**: Go somewhere quiet with time to yourself for half an hour. Use it to carry out a creative visualisation and imagine yourself in five years, living your best life. Get as specific as possible.

Where are you? Who are you with? How do you feel? What do you see and hear? What job are you doing? Where do you live? Who are you surrounded by?

Visualisation is a powerful tool for getting out of your present situation and asking yourself what could be possible. What do you want? 'What if?' is a powerful question to ask.

---

3. **Ask powerful questions**: Lisa Bean – a transformational coach and writer - suggests clarifying your purpose by writing down your answers to these three questions:

What change would you like to see in the world?
What do you wish you were free to do? What gifts can you use to make this happen?

You can combine these three answers to write your purpose in one sentence. **My purpose is…**

4. **Find your talents:** Try this quick version of Ikigai to help you find your unique gifts. Draw three columns on a sheet of paper and write '***What am I good at?***' on the left column; write down a quick list with at least ten things you are good at. On the right-hand column, write a similar list, but using the title, '***What do I love doing?***' Then in the centre column, write a list of things that are in both of the others. **What does it reveal to you about your talents?**

5. **What drives you? What are your values?** Your values are your personal principles or standards. Becoming more aware of these helps you understand what motivates you. According to Jinny Ditzler in her book *Your Best Year Yet!*, "What drives most of us is the ambition to improve the quality of our lives while being true to ourselves and what's important to us." Chapter five of her book contains powerful questions and exercises to help you explore your values. e.g., What values represent you? What values do you want to demonstrate? What do you want to happen due to your interaction with others? **Write down your top personal values below.** Also, try out this exercise from Brené Brown:

https://brenebrown.com/resources/dare-to-lead-list-of-values

What does the world need?

To help you find your purpose, one of the questions to ask yourself is: *What does the world need?* To be an effective changemaker, you must align your passions and skills with what is required for a sustainable world. You must develop the skills and qualities required for your green career. Here we explore two global sustainability frameworks, followed by practical exercises, to help you consider this more fully.

'*Think globally, act locally*' is an often-used slogan, originating from Friends of the Earth in 1971, the year I was born. When the earth's levels of carbon dioxide were around 325 parts per million, or ppm. Five decades later, that number – at the time of writing – is now 97 ppm higher at over 422 ppm. So, the idea urges us to consider the entire planet's health while taking action in our communities, as we clearly cannot solve these issues in our local communities alone. I like these two global frameworks as they provide inspiration, support, and tools for global and local action.

See what you think of them. How could they support your changemaker journey?

Sustainable Development Goals

The UN Sustainable Development Goals (SDG) comprise 17 global goals with a framework for achieving sustainability by 2030.

1. No poverty
2. Zero hunger
3. Good health and wellbeing
4. Quality education
5. Gender equality
6. Clean water and sanitation
7. Affordable and clean energy
8. Decent work and economic growth
9. Industry, innovation, and infrastructure
10. Reduced inequalities
11. Sustainable cities and communities
12. Responsible consumption and production
13. Climate action
14. Life below water

15. Life on land

16. Peace, justice, and strong institutions

17. Partnerships for the goals.

To find out more visit https://sdgs.un.org/goals

These interlinked goals aim to end poverty, hunger, and global heating. Partnerships are as equally important a goal as climate action; without them, it won't happen.

What goal(s) are most important to you?

Ask yourself:

What makes me angry?

What makes me passionate?

OR

What makes you happiest when you think of a world that has found that solution?

Catalyse Change is led by goal number 5. Achieve gender equality and empower all women and girls. As gender equality is a fundamental human right and a necessary foundation for a peaceful, prosperous, sustainable world. There has been progress over the last decades, but the world is not on track to achieve gender equality by 2030.

For me, it's also an equitable and fair world where people, regardless of gender or ethnicity, are free to live their best life. It doesn't mean I don't care about other things; you can be passionate
about many issues, but finding something that truly resonates with you can help guide your journey.

Inner development goals

The Sustainable Development Goals (SDG) have given us a blueprint for a sustainable world by 2030 – a vision and framework for what needs to happen.

However, progress has been slow and disappointing.

We have realised that our mindset and abilities must also be developed to deal with such complex social and environmental challenges.

The good news is that research shows we can create the inner abilities we need.

So, the Inner Development Goals (IDG) Initiative – a non-profit organisation for inner development – has been created to help us achieve sustainability. These are the key inner transformative or green skills you need for your green career.

What is the IDG framework?

A team of international researchers created it after an extensive consultation involving more than 1,000 people. It consists of five dimensions, with 23 skills and qualities, of human inner growth and development. These are:

Being: relationship to self. Cultivate your inner life and develop and deepen your relationship with your thoughts, feelings, and body. This helps you to be present, intentional, and non-reactive. The key skills required are: Inner Compass, Integrity and Authenticity, Openness and Learning Mindset, Self-awareness, and Presence.

Thinking: cognitive skills. Take different perspectives by developing your cognitive skills, evaluating information, and making sense of the world as an interconnected whole. This is essential for good decision-making. The key skills required are: Critical Thinking, Complexity Awareness, Perspective Skills, Sensemaking, Long-term Orientation, and

Visioning.

Relating: caring for others in the world.
Appreciating, caring for, and feeling connected to others – neighbours, future generations, or the biosphere – helps us create more sustainable and just systems and societies for everyone. Essential skills required are: Appreciativeness, Connectedness, Humility, Empathy, and Compassion.

Collaborating: social skills. To progress on shared concerns, you must develop your abilities to include holding space and communicating with stakeholders with different skills, values, and competencies. Essential skills required are: Communication, Co-creation, Inclusive Mindset and Intercultural Competence, Trust, and Mobilisation.

Acting: driving change. Qualities such as courage and optimism help you acquire true agency, generate original ideas, and persistently perform in uncertain times. The key skills required are Courage, Creativity, Optimism, and Perseverance.

Exercises

1. **Explore the SDGs.** What issue/s do you care about most? Which do you feel most passionately about? Journal your thoughts, feelings, and ideas about them. Can you talk these through with a friend, too? **Journal your thoughts, feelings and ideas about them.**

2. **Develop your green skills.** Can you think of an example where you have demonstrated each of the five IDG themes? Notice which ones you are stronger in and which ones you need to practise more. Focus on one where you aren't so comfortable and actively use it this week. **Capture your ideas and thoughts, and see what comes up.**

3. **Go daydream**. Daydreaming is another useful tool to help you find your purpose. Take time to reflect on what you cared about as a child. What did you enjoy doing most? How did it make you feel? This can help you tap into something you naturally gravitate towards but might not be aware of. Reflect on your memories and see where they lead. **Take your journal to capture your ideas and thoughts, and see what comes up for you.**

4. The joy review. As part of your daydreaming, think about three memorable times in your life when you have felt the greatest joy. Take time to immerse yourself in these memories and notice what comes up for you. **Journal your observations about these experiences, and notice any themes or commonalities between them.**

Grow your confidence

Confidence is vital for any changemaker. It provides a gateway to living your best life. Yet often, we don't have enough of it, or at least feel like we don't. But what is it exactly? Here we will explore what it is and why it is so important. Along with some tools to help you grow yours.

"The most beautiful thing you can wear is confidence."
Blake Lively, actress

Confidence is the feeling or belief that you can do something well or succeed at it.

We may have it sometimes, however, often it fades, gets knocked, and we feel vulnerable.

At other times, we don't even think about it, at those times, we can feel invincible.

We might be confident in one situation, while another makes us shy. And that's okay.

Similarly, there may be a stage or age, when you feel confident, but it can disappear.

It's a mysterious substance, this confidence –

where does it come from? Where can you get it? Can anyone get it? Are you born with it, or do you learn it?

The bad news is that women can find it harder to master than men.

According to Claire Zammit, a coach, teacher, and founder of *Feminine Power Academy:*

- Women create shame-based stories 80 percent more than boys and men.

- Women need to be 85 percent sure they can speak confidently – with men, it's around 35 percent.

- To apply for a job, a woman has to be over 80 percent confident she is qualified, whereas men are likely to apply even if they only meet around 60 percent of the requirements.

This isn't our fault.

We live in a patriarchal society where our culture supports the belief that men hold power.

This is on display to us daily, from who our leaders are, to how much we earn and how the media portrays us.

So, for women to have the same success and

opportunities that men enjoy, we must work harder to develop and demonstrate our confidence.

However, life is mirroring and matching how you show up.

To be an impactful changemaker, you have to expand and grow your confidence.

How do you do this?

Rhian Sherrington, a career coach who runs confidence workshops for Catalyse Change, shares her tips:

"Confidence is a skill that can be learned. It's a mindset, a set of behaviours and beliefs. Anyone can develop their confidence. Focusing on these three elements can help.

1. **Clarity**: Get clear on what confidence means to you. If you are seeking something, you must be clear on exactly what you are looking for. Confidence means different things to different people. Unpack what it means by considering what it feels, looks, behaves, and sounds like. Often, it's easier to start with what a lack of confidence is, so

you can start there and then switch around by asking yourself what would the opposite of that would feel, look, sound, and behave like?

2. **Competence**: You feel confident when you get good at something. We can spend too much time trying to work on our mind-talk, rather than simply looking at which of our skills, strengths, or activities to improve. Doing this could have the most significant impact on our feelings of self-confidence, so don't forget to develop your competencies in the places you need them.

3. **Courage:** As I talk about in my book, *Alchemy for the Mind, Create Your Confident Core*, having courage enables us to move through risk and uncertainty and do the things we want to do anyway. Each of us can do this, but we have our own personal scale as to what the fear or challenge is that we must overcome. Practising being courageous in small things (such as not apologising when it wasn't your fault or striking up a conversation with a stranger at the till) provides us with experiences that, with repeated exposure, lower our psychological fear response. This builds our capacity to take

courageous action where the stakes are higher, all of which develop our confidence."

Exercises

1. **Imagine your future self.** Use the previously explained creative visualisation technique on page 40 to imagine your ideal confident future self. Where are you, and who are you with? Spend some time exploring what you are doing and how that feels. **What are your top three qualities, and how do you express them? How can you be more like that now?**

_____

_____

_____

_____

_____

_____

_____

_____

_____

_____

_____

_____

_____

2. **Develop your competence**. Think about something you want to create. Reflect on where you currently doubt your ability to do it, then list some of your achievements, where you have already demonstrated these skills and abilities. How does this make you feel? What can you do to ensure you acknowledge your abilities and achievements regularly? **Next, write another list of the skills you need to work on to achieve it. What actions could you perform daily to help you develop your confidence in your skills and abilities?**

3. **Begin with the end in mind.** Before a meeting, imagine what you want to feel and achieve at the end of it. Athletes use this practice to help them win the race before they even go out on the track. Practise this for your next important or challenging conversation or activity. How does it make you feel? **What beliefs and behaviours do you have which might stop you? What could you do to change them?**

4. **Practice the 3 C's:** Clarity, Competence, and Courage. Which of these three do you need more practice in? What could you do to help you develop it? Start practising one of these as a daily activity this week and reflect on how it makes you feel. **Write below how this makes you feel and how you could use it to help you grow your confidence.**

5. **Power poses.** Next time you feel nervous, focus on your posture. A helpful technique is to hold your body in a strong position. Try the 'wonder woman' pose by looking straight ahead, with your hands on hips, feet slightly apart, chest and head lifted. Practise some strong ones now and see how it feels. Try them out before a meeting or presentation, ideally somewhere private!

Build your resilience

It's OK to feel anger, despair, or anxiety. It's a healthy response to this climate emergency we find ourselves in. Yet we still need to learn how to deal positively with these emotions. How do we build our resilience to help us survive and thrive as changemakers? What tools will help you cope effectively?

"Suffering from climate anxiety, depression, or grief isn't a mental disorder – it's a mark of one's connection to the world. It shows that you're able to empathize with people who are suffering and dying right now, and with the nonhuman creatures who are suffering with the whole world. It means you're not numbed by unconscious defenses – you're actually in touch with care for the world and feel it because horrible things are happening to our life support systems."

Dr Britt Wray, author and climate psychology expert

Flooding, droughts, forest fires. The signs of climate change are hard to miss. These 'once-in-a-lifetime' events are now happening daily. It's enough to make you feel anxious and to experience a deep dread about the future. You are not alone. Google searches for 'climate anxiety' soared 565 percent over twelve months from 2020 to 2021.

Climate - or eco-anxiety

In 2021, a global study[2] of 10,000 young people aged between 16 and 25 found that 45 percent said climate anxiety affected their daily lives. The United Nations and American Psychological Association say humans are increasingly at risk of climate-induced mental health issues.

Caroline Hickman, a researcher from the University of Bath Climate Psychology Alliance and a co-lead author of the study, said that anxiety among children was a, "Completely rational reaction given the inadequate responses to climate change they are seeing from governments."

Although eco or climate anxiety may not

---

[2] The study, which was said to be the first large-scale research of its kind, was led by academics from the UK's University of Bath and the Stanford Center for Innovation in Global Health, among others. It is under peer review in The Lancet Planetary Health journal.

constitute a mental illness, Caroline Hickman goes on to say, "The realities of climate change and government failures to act are chronic, long term and potentially inescapable stressors; conditions in which mental health problems will worsen."

"Eco-anxiety is emotional, mental or somatic distress in response to dangerous changes in the Climate System."

Climate Psychology Alliance

What is resilience?

Resilience is our ability to cope and recover from setbacks and difficulties. It is the outcome and process of successfully adapting to challenging life experiences.

Katie Hodgetts of The Resilience Project says, "Our ability to feel resilient is how we weather the storms. It is not about the absence of storms."

She compares having inner resilience to wearing a rucksack which is sometimes full, sometimes empty, but always there. "Nothing blooms all year round; neither will you."

What support is available?

Ecoanxiety is a serious and vast topic that I can't cover fully here. Fortunately, a lot of useful support is available, from books to podcasts to support organisations. Please take a look at the resources section at the back for some recommendations of where to find out more.

Five tips to help you

When you feel stressed and anxious, many exercises are proven to help. We all know that eating well and getting enough sleep makes us feel better, but how often do we act on it? It's easy to procrastinate and put things off, e.g., promising ourselves to go to the gym or eat less junk food just as soon as we get through exams, a break-up, the holidays, etc. However, as with most new habits, the best time to start is now. Which one of these five activities could you try today?

Start talking. Clover Hogan, climate activist and founder of youth organisation *Force of Nature*, says we should talk about these feelings rather than run away from them, as eco-anxiety is a rational, essential response to seeing the climate crisis play out around the world. She says, "What we need is people who are awake, people who are experiencing those feelings, rather than shutting down from them." *So try sharing your worries about climate change with friends and family. Journalling your thoughts and feelings can help too.*

Breathe. Simple deep breathing is one of the most effective ways to deal with anxiety. Neuroscientist Wendy Suzuki shares two evidence-based activities, breathing and movement, in her Ted Talk that can soothe your nervous system and fuel creativity and connection. She recommends using a box-breathing technique which involves breathing in deeply through your nose for four counts, holding onto your breath for four counts, exhaling deeply for four counts, then four more counts after you exhale. *Can you add this to your daily routine? Can you try using it before a meeting, exam, or other activity that makes you nervous?*

Get moving. When you move your body, beneficial neurochemicals are released in your brain. This increases positive mental states and decreases negative ones. It immediately positively affects your body and is even more helpful when combined with other personal development and spiritual practices. So, find something you enjoy and do it regularly. Whether running, swimming, or walking in the park, make it part of your daily routine. *Try starting the day with ten minutes of exercise, e.g., aerobics, dance, or yoga. Record any noticeable effects after doing this for a day, a week, and a month.*

Be mindful. Everything starts with your mind. Daily meditation or mindfulness practices help you stay calm and focused. They allow you to bring awareness to your thoughts. Use them to catch and deal with anxious thoughts as they come up. These thoughts can start innocently enough but soon spiral. Mindfulness helps you do something about them before they take hold. *Try using an app to help you, e.g., Calm, Insight Timer, or Headspace, or one of the many YouTube meditation videos. Journal about this experience.*

Take action. This is one of the best ways to confront climate anxiety. Research shows that engaging in collective environmental action – like outreach or advocacy – helps to reduce stress and anxiety. *Find other like-minded people and groups and engage in activities that feel good to you. Join an environmental or campaigning group you support – check out the resource section at the back for ideas.*

Reframe your story

We all create narratives about who we are, what we deserve, and what we are capable of.
What stories are you telling yourself? Which ones aren't serving you?

How can you change the stories where you are unworthy of success or happiness, so they support rather than sabotage you? Here, we explore how you can challenge your current unhelpful narratives.

> *"Whether you think you can or can't – you are right."*
> **Henry Ford, industrialist & businessperson**

Reframing is about shifting the lens to reframe what you perceive and experience. Those experiences we hold onto from our upbringing, society, and those of our own making. It is a standard tool used in psychology and is an essential one for a changemaker.

Change your mind

'Growth mindset' is the belief that your intelligence
and abilities can be developed through effort,
practice, and the right learning strategies. Psychologist
Professor Carol Dweck coined this term when
researching how people's underlying beliefs about
themselves can affect their lives.

People with a growth mindset believe they can
learn from challenges and setbacks – that they have
the constant potential for growth, change, and
improvement. They believe their natural intelligence
and talent are not a fixed limit but a starting point that
can improve over time.

The opposite of this is a 'fixed mindset', where you
take failure as evidence that you are not good at
something. People with a fixed mindset are more
likely to believe their abilities can't be changed and
they either have a gift for it or not. They're usually
easily discouraged and might avoid taking risks or
trying new things because they fear failure.

Changing the way you think takes time. However,
you can learn to reframe your thoughts through
practise and persistence. You can change negative

thoughts into positive ones by working with your mental processes.

Our brains lie

We often assume our thoughts are true, yet we are all susceptible to unhealthy thought patterns. These are known as cognitive distortions.

When our emotions get involved, our brains can lie and warp reality.

Cognitive Behavioural Therapy – the evidence-based psychotherapy treatment – is focused on changing negative thoughts and behaviours. It uses reframing to correct the negative thinking patterns that hurt us and help us look at things differently.

Believe it's possible

Amazing things can happen. Once you change the conversation you have with yourself.

What do you tell yourself about your potential? Can you challenge yourself to rethink your beliefs and limitations to shape the future you want by being purposeful?

- Have a vision for yourself and set intentions.

- Train your brain to see what is possible.

- Start to learn how to identify and deal with negative thoughts.

- Become aware of them and ask yourself if they are trustworthy or helpful.

- Try to remember and celebrate your successes instead.

- Use creative visualisation to imagine the life you really want to create.

When you start to retell the same old stories, e.g., that you are not good enough, or start to worry about what others will think, try reframing them. Here are some practices to help.

Exercises

1. **Notice your thoughts.** When you feel a strong emotion like anxiety, stop yourself and ask, '*What am I thinking right now?*' Then write it down. It will show you what you could reframe and provides a record of your thinking patterns over time. You can reduce your anxiety just by acknowledging and writing your thoughts down. **Try doing this now using a recent thought that has been bothering you.**

2. **Reframe your weaknesses.** What are your top five strengths? If you find it difficult, consider what your colleagues or friends might say about you. Then think about how these strengths can sometimes have a negative impact, if used too often, too intensely, or at the wrong time, e.g., *self-confidence can become arrogance, ambition becomes ruthlessness, and trusting becomes gullible.* Write down examples of how this might be true for your top strengths. *Now think about your five most annoying weaknesses. How could you now reframe them as strengths?* **Write down any insights you have from doing this.**

3. **Learn from your successes.** How have you turned negative thoughts around in the past? Think about when you last had a negative thought. What did you do to eliminate it? Then reflect on times when you have brought awareness to negative thoughts and managed to deflect or turn them around. **Write some examples of things that have helped you stop negative thoughts in the past.**

4. **What would you say to a friend?** When you next have a negative thought you can't get rid of, think about what you would say to a friend who came to you with this problem. Doing this can help you reframe your thoughts and escape your negative self-talk loop. **Reflect and capture your thoughts and learnings.**

5. **Where are you stuck?** Think about an area of your life where you are stuck. Be honest and think about what or who you blame for your situation. What's the old story there? Try to let it go and look for what happens inside that story. What's the pattern that keeps happening in this area of your life? Think about your thoughts and behaviours in this situation. *Are you showing up in a way that creates evidence for why this situation can't change? What new behaviours could you start now to help to change it?*

Write out this story with your observations.

SECTION 3:

THE JOURNEY: BECOMING A CHANGEMAKER

Green careers

Imagine having a career you enjoy. One which also makes the world a better place. How do you go about finding this? What are the opportunities and pathways available for you to achieve it? Here we explore the skills, knowledge, and experiences you need to get that dream green career.

Green or climate jobs focus on sustainability through environmental protection and/or social responsibility.

They are jobs that contribute to 'happy, healthy, and green communities and the planet'.

These can be defined either by the job or the employers' nature and purpose.

The good news is that every job now has the potential to be a 'green' one.

"Inside most companies, only a handful of people with 'sustainability' roles consider climate issues part of their workday. But in this most all-encompassing challenge in human history, every job must be a climate job." **Project Drawdown**

Traditionally, green jobs have just described those with a direct, positive impact on the environment, e.g., renewable energy, conservation, or sustainable transport. However, as society transitions to low-carbon models, it has opened up the number of opportunities available.

A job can be considered green if it has a 'net-positive impact' on society and the environment. This means putting more back than you take out by prioritising the health and well-being of our people and planet over making a profit. Yet there is no one universally agreed definition.

The Office for National Statistics (ONS) says:
"Employment in an activity that contributes to protecting or restoring the environment, including those that mitigate or adapt to climate change."

The United Nations Environment Programme says:
"The green economy is one that results in improved human well-being and social equity while significantly reducing environmental risks and ecological scarcities. A green economy can be thought of as one which is low-carbon, resource-efficient,

and socially inclusive."

Whatever the final definition, we can all agree that this transition to a circular economy will require a different mindset and skillset for the new emerging jobs. It also means making changes to existing roles, so they are more sustainable too.

To respond quickly and effectively to our ecological and social emergencies, we need motivated, resilient, and skilled changemakers – now more than ever.

Growing opportunities

Globally, the number of green jobs has grown by eight percent per year in the past five years. The World Economic Forum predicts the global green economy will create more than 10.3 million new jobs by 2030, meaning that green career opportunities are only likely to increase.

Research suggests that one in five jobs in the UK (approximately 6.3 million workers) are likely to be affected positively or negatively by the transition to a green economy. This will lead to increased jobs as long as those at risk can be upskilled appropriately.

*"The number of UK-based jobs in low-carbon and renewable energy sectors in 2021 was almost 40,000 higher than in 2020, official new figures show. But the Government is still not on track to deliver its flagship pledge of two million green jobs by 2030." **Edie.net***

LinkedIn, the business and social online platform, says, 'Sustainability Manager' is the second-fastest growing job title across the UK, with Sustainability Analyst and Specialist also in their top ten. However, data from LinkedIn also shows that environmentally relevant opportunities are now also showing up in sectors not traditionally seen as green.

As the green economy is still in its infancy the transition from 'business-as-usual' to a new sustainable economy is opening up many new opportunities. This will likely continue for years as new clean technologies, policies, and standards are adopted.

Making sense of this new, low-carbon economy can take time and effort. However, it means you have many options if you're committed to finding a career that will positively impact the planet.

Trends shaping the economy

1. Demand for green talent will soon outpace supply.
2. Hiring of green talent is accelerating faster than overall hiring.
3. There's currently a good balance in the sought-after green skills.
4. The fastest-growing green skills are both mainstream and emerging.
5. The volume of workers moving into green and greening jobs is too low.

Green jobs update

LinkedIn analysis shows that many of the fastest-growing green jobs involve non-traditional roles.

Traditional green jobs

Occupation	Average number of green skills required	Annual growth in number of job postings in 2020
Environmental Consultant	4.2	18%
Sustainability Manager	3.8	1%
Health Safety Environment Engineer	3.3	19%
Solar Consultant	2.9	4%
Energy Consultant	3.3	10%

Nontraditional green jobs

Occupation	Average number of green skills required	Annual growth in number of job postings in 2020
Business Consultant	3.3	35%
Program Manager	2.8	53%
Compliance Manager	2.5	10%
Sales Manager	2.8	31%
Customer Service Manager	2.6	33%

Linked**in**
News

When will this happen?

We need a decarbonised economy far sooner than 2050.

To help us, Kate Raworth has created 'Doughnut

Economics', an economic model which balances essential human needs with existing planetary boundaries. Kate says, "…we should redesign our economy to a circular model. One which recycles rather than wastes resources. This requires creativity and innovation to ensure products can be repaired, remade, and repurposed."

We need to start now.

A just transition

The shift to a low-carbon and sustainable society must be as equitable as possible; it must be a 'just transition.'

Polluting jobs, such as those in gas and oil, will have to disappear to support our transition to net zero.

However, they must be replaced with greener ones to avoid mass unemployment.

We must create a 'just transition' where nobody is left behind.

This isn't just about the most obvious jobs. Every job has the potential to become green.

Social sustainability too

We must also integrate social sustainability into this just and green transition. Existing definitions often miss out on the social aspect – such as the PwC Green Jobs Barometer 2022 – yet there are three pillars of sustainability.

The International Labour Organisation says that most definitions 'incorporate the most holistic approach of sustainable development.' This means that social justice is also included in most definitions of a green economy.

Rhian Sherrington, the founder of Women in Sustainability, says, "Women are still under-represented in the construction/energy/utilities areas of 'green jobs', but as soon as you include the social and consider the massive contributions from say 'carbon neutral' jobs – such as in care, health, education, social work, the whole landscape changes. And given that all jobs are sustainability jobs (or need to be very shortly), let's take the opportunity to envision and deliver an economy focused around purpose, enabling the flourishing of life – human and ecological well-being the ultimate goal."

Green skills

The transition to a green economy requires new skills.
Green skills are the knowledge, abilities, values, and
attitudes needed to live in, develop, and support a
sustainable and resource-efficient society.

*"It's more than jobs—we need to zoom in on the skills that
power these jobs. Green skills. We believe real change will come
through a skills-based approach to opportunity. We have seen
double-digit growth across dozens of green skills over the last
five years. The fastest-growing green skills are in Ecosystem
Management, Environmental Policy, and Pollution Prevention.
But most green skills are used in jobs that aren't traditionally
considered green—fleet managers, data scientists, or health
workers."* **Ryan Roslansky, CEO, LinkedIn**

The Green General Skill Index identifies four work
tasks that are particularly important for green
occupations: Engineering and Technical skills, Science
skills, Operational and Management skills, and
Monitoring skills. A range of soft skills are vital, too.

Skills gaps and shortages are already recognised as
a problem in critical sectors, such as digital, energy

and resource efficiency, construction, engineering, environmental services, renewable energy, and manufacturing. While the United Nations Environment Programme highlights that the green economy will require talent across all business areas.

Widening skills gap

The UK Environmental Audit Committee has warned of a 'skills gap' across all sectors that threatens to undermine critical targets in the government's 25-year environment plan.

The good news is that to meet the required supply and demand, and global net zero goals, green skills must increase in every industry and country.

New opportunities are appearing across all sectors as demand outstrips supply.

In-demand skills include sustainable development, environmental policy, and environmental remediation.

However, analysis by LinkedIn shows that green skills are starting to appear in sectors that aren't traditionally considered to be green, e.g., sustainable fashion, business management, and sales. Around 10 percent of LinkedIn job postings in 2021 expressly required at least one green skill.

In fact, over the past five years, job postings requiring green skills grew eight percent each year, yet the amount of green talent available has only grown at roughly six percent per year.

This provides an excellent opportunity for you to succeed in your dream green career.

Different job categories:

Dark Green Jobs (technical): These relate directly to the delivery of sustainability or environmental jobs in a corporate, consultancy, or other organisation, e.g., sustainability consultant, ESG reporting expert, ethical supply chain expert, and energy manager.

Light Green Jobs (transferrable): These represent a broader category within many career types. They are positions created due to sustainability market forces, which allow a much broader range of educational backgrounds. They aren't hired for specific sustainability knowledge but for an ancillary skillset, e.g., marketing consultant, sales and business manager, HR manager, business development manager, and administrator.

Top 10 skills and categories

Top in-demand skills, required by employers, via LinkedIn.

1. Sustainability - Sustainable Development

2. Remediation - Environmental Remediation

3. Occupational Health and Safety Officer - Environmental Policy

4. Climate - Ecosystem Management

5. Renewable Energy - Renewable Energy Generation

6. Environmental Awareness - Ecosystem Management

7. Environmental Health & Safety (EHS) - Environmental Auditing

8. Solar Energy - Renewable Energy Generation

9. Corporate Social Responsibility (CSR) - Environmental Policy

10. Recycling - Environmental Remediation.

Fastest-growing green jobs

LinkedIn looks at the percentage of jobs listed that require green skills, here are some examples of the fastest growing ones. Refer to their online Global Green Skills report for the most recent updates.

Business consultancy, programme management, sales, and customer services are significant growth areas. Green-related job postings in those fields rose 30 percent or more in the EU/UK.

There's also growth in traditional green occupations such as environmental consultants, energy consultants, and environmental health and safety engineers. These jobs typically call for at least three to four explicit green skills.

So, there are many opportunities, and they are rapidly growing. But how do you get there?

What could this look like in practice?

We invite a diverse selection of women - who work in Sustainability and ESG (Environmental Social Governance) roles - to talk at our Catalyse Change events. To help inspire and inform you, here are a few examples of their green careers and the pathways into them.

Amelia is a Community Renewables Engagement

Lead for Younity, an organisation specialising in community energy. In addition, she works part-time in environmental communications for Earth Minutes and is a youth advisor and board member for several environmental groups. Her first job was as CRM Marketing Assistant at Ecotricity, the renewable energy company, which led to a community energy role with Midcounties Cooperative and Younity. She didn't previously have technical skills in energy, so she advises, *"If you don't understand something, it shouldn't restrict you. Your personal drivers will help you learn and develop skills on the job."*

Jen is Co-owner and Director of Poco Tapas Bar, a restaurant in the centre of Bristol committed to operating sustainably. The Sustainable Restaurant Association awarded them Sustainable Restaurant of the Year in 2016 and 2018. She has also recently trained as a yoga teacher too. At University, Jen studied politics, philosophy, and economics and had yet to gain business experience but figured it out as she went along. She says, *"Part of our motivation for opening Poco was to be a part of the industry shift away from wasteful kitchens, mistreated staff and distant supply chains, towards a conscious, holistic and environmentally minded business.*"

Kate is a Responsible Business Consultant and Advisor. She now runs Green Unlimited, a consultancy helping organisations develop sustainable business strategies and communicate with stakeholders. Before working for herself, she worked for four environmental/sustainability consultancies and in-house for an international environmental charity. She advises that essential skills for being a consultant are, "*Listening, being organised, and being at least one step ahead.*"

Kirsty is Group Head of Sustainability for Hays, a global recruitment agency, where she develops and drives their sustainability and broader ESG strategy in alignment with purpose and values. She was previously Head of Corporate Sustainability at the law firm Burges Salmon. Her skills and experience have been built over many years. She has academic qualifications, including an MSc in Engineering and an MBA in Business but says that work experience and personal development are the most important things. "*I think the biggest thing is attitude – be curious, learn from others, lean into opportunities, go above and beyond, know your boundaries, and recognise we never stop learning.*"

Megan is a Marketing & Communications Manager for Force of Nature, a youth non-profit transforming mindsets for climate action. Her pathway into this was through an internship with a purpose-led social media agency, which led to a job delivering digital campaigns for Greenhouse Communications. Her top tips for getting your dream green career are, "*Build your LinkedIn profile, make sure it's up to date, and consider applying speculatively to a company you love.*"

Vibhati is a Managing Sustainability Consultant for Energise, developing social sustainability services including B impact assessments, human rights and supply chain assessments, diversity, equity, and inclusion strategy, and audits, alongside social and environmental justice campaigning. She is also the Founder of South Asians for Sustainability, an organisation raising awareness about the climate emergency among South Asian communities in a culturally relevant way and bridging the diversity gap in the sector. She shared her top tips for achieving a desired career, "*Everything you learn on your journey, every person you meet or network with, and every conversation you have is worthwhile and never wasted. You gain technical and soft skills from all aspects of your life – take time to analyse your personality, map out your strengths, and the areas you may want to improve or build on. Define what success means to you and how your career can support the long-term lifestyle you'd like to lead rather than chasing a job title or salary. Absorb all you can from your surroundings and mentors along the way and always lead with your best intentions.*"

Resources to help you

To understand what this could look like for you in the real world, check out some online resources to guide you.

EAUC: The Alliance for Sustainability Leadership in Education has a range of excellent online resources, including career webinars. A good place to start is with their comprehensive eBook, *'EAUC Sustainability Careers Guide,'* which has links to their webinars and a range of other useful resources.

https://www.eauc.org.uk/sustainability_careers_guide

Prospects: A wide range of text-based career profiles, including a large section under Environment and Agriculture, which often refer to sustainability, as do those under Energy and Utilities and Public Services and Administration. https://www.prospects.ac.uk/

Target Jobs: They list many jobs you can go through and allow you to select an area to focus on. You will need to search subject areas related to sustainability that interest you (e.g., environment, conservation, waste). https://targetjobs.co.uk/careers-advice/job-descriptions

The National Careers Service for the UK: They also provide outlines for many job options.

https://nationalcareers.service.gov.uk/explore-careers

Catalyse Change: Green career blogs from women working in sustainability help provide insights into various opportunities and pathways. Follow on

Instagram - @catalysechange - for regular updates.

https://catalysechange.com/

Go to the resources section at the back of this book for more details about these and other organisations that can help you.

Different pathways

You don't need fancy qualifications, specialist technical knowledge, or loads of experience to work in sustainability. You can play your part in many ways. However, a good education will give you a great head start, providing you with the knowledge, skills, and opportunities to make a difference. In fact, it is normally now a baseline requirement, even for entry-level jobs. Or perhaps you would prefer to take a more practical pathway through an apprenticeship?

University and other higher education

There is now a vast selection of environmental and sustainability-focused bachelor's and master's degrees at universities in the UK and worldwide.

Whether you want to become a campaigner, conservationist, soil scientist, or sustainability consultant, you can gain the knowledge and skills you need to land your desired job. They will give you an advantage when job hunting in today's sustainability job market.

There is an incredibly diverse range of courses and disciplines out there, from Business, Conservation, Earth Science, Ecology, Energy, Environmental Management, Geography, International Relations, Sustainable Development, and Urban Planning.

There are several different types of degrees, so you must decide which is best for you and your career goals. Each provides different career opportunities you might want to consider before choosing one degree over another.

- **Associate's degree**: An associate's degree programme aims to provide students with the skills and education they need to begin a career. This undergraduate degree typically takes two to three years to complete.

- **Bachelor's degree:** A bachelor's degree is increasingly considered the minimum for entry-level positions for sustainability jobs. They are normally carried out for three or four years. You are an undergraduate if you are studying for your first degree – usually a Bachelor of Arts (BA) or Bachelor of Science (BSc).

- **Master's degree:** A master's can help you

advance professionally in many careers, such as sustainability manager or director. Most are one or two years long. Many post-graduate degrees are available online, and some offer flexible schedules.

Catalyse Change has produced a guide to many of these, which you can download from their website. Shared below are two different experiences from their alums. Also, research university websites to learn about all the current options available.

*"When researching and exploring the different options for studying a degree in sustainability, I quickly realised how broad the topic is. So many approaches to finding solutions to climate change gave me hope for the future. For anyone considering applying for a degree in sustainability explore your interests and focus within that field, as the options are almost never-ending. Participating in the Catalyse Change Summit helped me with this, as I heard from professionals working in many different fields of sustainability. And talking with my mentor gave me the clarity I needed to isolate my main interest, sustainability consultancy." **Lara, Catalyse Change alumni***

"I applied to Cambridge University as there was a course I wanted to study, Human, Social, and Political Sciences, which is studied with three departments: politics, anthropology, and sociology, but intersects with issues such as colonialism, racism, and sexism.

As a Visible Minority Ethnic (VME) person, nobody in my family had been to Oxbridge. My sixth-form head helped with my personal statement and submitting a piece of work, but nobody else supported me, especially with my assessment and interview. Other pupils received one-to-one tuition for their assessments, but I was just given a link to the past papers. I had one mock interview in school, with the very old, retired ex-head who was too kind and too out of date. I got rejected, I was devastated and could not go through that again.

In the following October, during my lockdown gap year, I realised that I could overcome my disappointment and decided to re-apply to Cambridge but to a different college, despite my head teacher trying to put me off by telling me that nobody gets into Cambridge on a second application. For my second application, I read lots of books, re-wrote essays, found teachers at other schools to mark them as my teachers wouldn't. I also contacted people who had been to Cambridge in the last ten years and persuaded them to do mock interviews with me, and prepared well. I also had mock interviews and prep with someone who was head of sixth form at a London school. He gave me reading, pushed me hard and made me focus on sociology, my weakest subject but his degree subject.

I also got feedback from university lecturers that I knew, who suggested issues that I needed to cover in my interview. I also applied to the Sutton Trust, who support VME people, and attended helpful webinars. I gave it my best shot and knew, whether I got in or not, I had no remorse. This time I was offered a place at Cambridge University at St John's College which is one of the best known colleges. So, the only advice I can give is don't give up, and if you can give it another shot, try again. Also, don't rely totally on your teachers or school, as racism and stereotyping can act as a barrier for VME pupils, and contact the Sutton Trust who might be able to help."

Mya-Rose Craig, author of Birdgirl, student, and activist. Also a Catalyse Change alum and ambassador.

Internships

An internship is a period of work experience a company offers for a limited time. They can be useful for helping you decide what career you want to pursue, while also providing valuable experience and content for your CV. Here is some advice from Maddy Diment based on a blog she wrote for Catalyse Change from her experiences of internships.

Begin by answering the following questions: *What would an 'ideal' internship look like for me? Where would it be based, how long would it be, and do I have any specific requirements? What skills do I want to learn or develop? In which industry do I want to gain insight? What are my values, and how does it reflect them?*

Research:

- **Research available internships** so you can make strategic decisions.
- **Talk to the National Careers Service**, or the one at your school or university, and ask for recommendations.
- **Search broad key search terms** via Google and LinkedIn, e.g., 'Sustainability Summer Internship', and see what appeals to you.

Speculative opportunities: An advertised internship

has obvious benefits: they tend to be well-structured and may even lead to a full-time position in the company. However, they are also very competitive. So why not directly contact an organisation you are interested in and see what they can offer?

First, you should prepare a few points:

Why are you interested in working for them? What makes them unique and meaningful to you, unlike their competitors or other companies you like?

What can you offer them? Have you identified a need in their company that you can fulfil? Where is your evidence for the skills you claim to have?

How would you like the internship to look? Write down your essential requirements, e.g., hybrid or in an office? Full or part time? Two or eight weeks? Write down your basic needs (including payment) to prepare you for negotiations.

The process: Send off your emails and attach a tailored CV and cover letter. If you don't get a response, try not to take it personally. Some businesses (particularly small ones) may not be able to respond to every email, let alone be able to offer you an internship. However, don't be afraid to chase them up via email or give them a call.

Once you have secured your internship, make the most of the opportunity.

Here are a few tips:

Set goals: Write down a list of goals you want to achieve, e.g., learn a specific skill, understand the industry better, or practice public speaking.

Keep an internship diary: You will learn a lot during your internship – about yourself, the company, and the industry – so keep a record of your findings. This will help you to write future CVs and answer behavioural interview questions.

Build relationships: Life is all about building and maintaining relationships, and an internship is no different. Ask as many questions as possible and try to get to know colleagues. You never know where these connections will lead you.

"These tips helped me secure three internships, which I co-created – one in academia, one in a small business, and one in luxury retail. For two of the organisations, I did not know anyone who currently works, or historically worked, there. For the other one, I had a friend who interned there the summer prior, so I could ask her how she found it, etc."

Maddie Diment, researcher.

Green apprenticeships

Apprenticeships are a system for teaching new practitioners of a trade or profession, providing on-the-job training alongside study. They are currently having a resurgence with lots of new support and options now available. Could this be a green career pathway for you?

"In 2022 in the UK, there were 70 apprenticeships that are now supportive of green or net zero goals, with well over 100 existing apprenticeships also up for revision to make them greener. These include sustainability business specialists, ecologists, countryside rangers, and forest craftspeople. They have been updated by employers to ensure they fit the economy's emerging green skills needs, with support from the IfATE."

Institute for Apprenticeships and Technical Education (IfATE)

Apprenticeships provide an excellent option for people of all ages to break into the green sector. They offer the opportunity to earn while you learn, with the option to train up to a degree level. There are lots of green apprenticeships available, from environmental consultancy and business sustainability to forestry and wind turbine technology.

Different shades of green

- **Light green**: The nature of the work is unchanged by green requirements, but it may have additional duties done sustainably, e.g., florist, marketing assistant.

- **Mid green**: The job remains the same, but there might be a need for new knowledge, skills, and behaviours for using new technologies, e.g., engineer or transport planner.

- **Dark green**: A role embedded within the green occupational landscape and delivering sustainable outcomes, e.g., wind turbine engineer, recycling operative.

What could this look like in practice?

- **Electrician**: As well as all the traditional skills for this trade, this apprenticeship now trains people to install and maintain domestic heat pumps, solar panels, and electric vehicle charging points.

- **Forest craftsperson**: To carry out the practical operations required to create, maintain and harvest forests and woodlands.

- **Sustainability business specialist**: To help organisations to manage the resources they use and the waste they generate according to environmentally friendly principles.

Exercises

1. **Do some online research**. Explore the different options and support available.

2. **Chat with an adviser**. A career adviser can help you choose the best option for you.

3. **Try a Skills Bootcamp first**. These are flexible courses of up to 16 weeks, allowing you to gain sector-specific skills, including electric vehicles, green heating technology, smart metre installation, and the offer of a job interview.

Record your thoughts and actions below.

Be a solutionist!

If you are struggling to get into sustainability, what other options exist? Here are a few more ideas you could explore:

1. **Make any job green**: Why not take an entry-level job in any industry and drive sustainability changes from the inside? This will enable you to develop valuable transferable experience and skills while proving yourself to be a leader and a problem solver – both vital, sought after sustainability skills. Many organisations already have informal working groups which focus on social or environmental sustainability, so you could join one of them or - if there isn't one already - then why not set one up?

2. **Be an ecopreneur**: Ever wanted to work for yourself? First, you need to identify a problem that needs solving and one you want to solve. Do some market research to find out if there is a gap in the market and who else is already out there. Just know, this can be risky and tough. However, many organisations, such as The Prince's Trust and The

School for Social Entrepreneurs, provide free support to help you get started. See the resources section.

3. **Volunteer**: Even if your job isn't sustainability focused, you can still make a difference. Contact local charities, environmental groups, or activist campaigns to see how you can help. You will gain valuable skills, experience, and networks in the process. There are often volunteering opportunities at all levels, even as a charity Trustee, where you can learn management and decision-making skills too.

Solitaire Townsend, the entrepreneur who wrote, *The Solutionists, How Business Can Fix the Future*, says "… to succeed in sustainability you need to be a 'Solutionist' or problem solver…" She continues, "Don't wait for the perfect sustainability job description to land in your inbox; it might never happen. Solutionists operate at the very forefront of society's response to the world's biggest challenges, which means traditional job roles often can't keep up with us."

Understand yourself better

Job and career opportunities in sustainability are growing across all fields. But how do you choose one which is best suited to your unique skills and strengths? What are the next steps to landing your dream green career?

How well do you know yourself?

The better you know yourself, the better placed you will be to align your interests, skills, and abilities with the world of work. Personality tests can help you to explore this. They can also help you make improved subject and career choices, provide insights into your mental health, and improve how you work with others and in a team.

What are your top strengths?

Understanding yourself better will help you make sound decisions about your education and career paths. It also allows you to think about the subjects and activities you enjoy and excel at. Which of these types of strengths do you identify with most?

Thinking: Analytical (logic, objective, critical thinking), common sense, creativity, curiosity, detail focus, reflection, strategic mindedness.

Emotional: Courage, drive, emotional awareness, enthusiasm, optimism, persistence, resilience, self-confidence.

Communicating & influencing: Collaboration, communicator, developer, fairness, humour, inclusion, leader, listener, motivator, persuasive, relationship builder, writer.

Action & execution: Adaptability, decisiveness, efficiency, organiser, initiative, problem-solver, results-focused, self-improvement.

Tools which can help you:

- **Myers Briggs Type Indicator (MBTI)**: A tool to help you identify your personality type, strengths, and preferences. Developed by Isabel Myers and her mother, Katherine Briggs, based on Carl Jung's theory of personality types. Today it is one of the world's most widely used psychological instruments. Allowing you to understand your personality better. The test covers likes, dislikes, strengths, weaknesses, career preferences, and compatibility with others.

- **Free online tests: 16 Personality Test**: To help you understand your personality better using the MBTI 16 different types. **Truity**: Also measures your preferences using MBTI along with 23 more detailed facets of type to personalise your results.

- **Organisation tools**: CliftonStrengths Assessment and DISC are tools which you can pay to use, they are often used within businesses to support better team working.

- **C-me Profiling**: C-me focuses on behaviour rather than personality, as our behaviour impacts our reactions to situations and interactions. At Catalyse Change, we run an interactive workshop using this tool and approach within our Green Career training.

Exercises

1. **What problems do you want to solve?** The opportunities in sustainability are vast, so find which topics interest you most. Think about how you currently spend most of your time. What industry and roles inspire you? What hobbies or projects have engaged you in life so far? These are all excellent indicators of where your passions lie. Look at the UN Sustainable Development Goals for inspiration. **Create a top 10 list of the sustainability issues that most excite you and prioritise which ones to research.**

2. **What do you enjoy?** Sustainability is multi-disciplinary and can be embedded into almost any career. So, choose something you enjoy and are good at. First, list all your different skills and interests, use a piece of flip chart paper or a whiteboard to create a comprehensive list or mind map. Can you see any themes appearing? Any connections you hadn't thought of before? Don't leave anything out, however small or silly it might seem. Everything is relevant to understanding where your natural skills and interests lie. **Now think about all the possible career ideas based on your top 10 skills and interests.**

3. **Research the various degree courses, traineeships, internships, or college courses available to support your career pathway into these and their entry-level requirements.**

4. **Set goals.** Define your ultimate vision or goal. Then work backward to determine what you must do to achieve it. Try using the GROW model to help you. It is a simple system used in coaching to help you work through your goal and determine how to achieve it.

G - Goal: What is the endpoint where you want to be? Does this goal fit with your overall career objectives? What are all the parts that make up your goal? Make sure that this is a SMART goal: Specific, Measurable, Attainable, Realistic, and Time-bound.

R - Reality: Where are you right now? What have you done already, and what have you learned? What might stop you from achieving your goal? What happens now (what, who, when, and how often)? What is the effect or result of this? Have you already taken any steps toward your goal? Does this goal conflict with any other plans or objectives?

O - Options: What could you do to achieve your goal? What are the advantages and disadvantages of each option? What do you need to stop doing to achieve this goal? What obstacles stand in your way?

Conjure up as many good options as possible, then review these and decide the best ones.

W - Way forward: What actions you are now going to take? What will you do now, and when? What else will you do? What could stop you from moving forward? How will you overcome this? How can you keep yourself motivated? When do you need to review progress? Daily, weekly, monthly?

5. Create an action plan to help you set and deliver your Green Career Goals.

CV writing tips

A CV (or resumé) is essential for getting an interview for your dream green job. A good CV makes all the difference in a highly competitive marketplace. However, writing it can be stressful, especially if you have never done so before. Here are a few tips to help.

"It takes just seven seconds for an employer to accept or reject a CV – so make sure yours stands out."
James Reed, Chair, Reed Recruitment

There is no perfect format. However, you should follow some basic rules. Think about your CV as a marketing document. It shows an employer why you are the person who can solve their problems. Why you will be an asset to their organisation and team. Ensure it is personal to you – write in the first person – and that it stands out to give you the edge.

What to include

1. **Structure**: Start with a summary of your personal details, work experience, and achievements. Order your experience and education with the most recent first.

2. **Punchy opening paragraph**: Start with a personal statement – or summary about yourself – stating who you are, what you can offer, and your career goals. Make it engaging and exciting, use an active voice, and keep your sentences short.

3. **Keywords**: Use strong keywords or phrases, e.g., confident, proactive, proven, track-record, experienced, delivering results. Always back them up with evidence.

4. **Be specific**: Quantify and measure your impact where you can, including examples of how you added value. *What was the outcome, and who did you impact?*

5. **Simple format**: Use the whole space across the two pages, i.e., no columns, borders, or pictures. Choose a clear, professional font so it is easy to read.

6. **Short and concise**: It should be no more than two pages of A4 to scan and read quickly. If printing, do so double-sided. Use bullet points, including an action and a result with each.

7. **Use the job description**: Refer to the skills specified in the job description and/or person specification to ensure you make it clear why you are a perfect fit for the role.

8. **Avoid clichés and jargon**: Make it as personal and engaging as possible, with specific examples that are easy to understand.

9. **Tailor it**: Depending on the job you are applying for, ensure your CV reflects the job description and specifications.

10. **Unique selling point**: What is yours, and have you got it across?

Cover letter

For most jobs, the cover letter is your chance to stand out. Some of the same rules apply to the CV, e.g.,

- Covering no more than one page, make it clear and engaging by using an active voice, bullets, and headers to make points stand out.

- Use the 'rule of three' so you don't fit in too much, e.g., pick three critical skills – which the job description requires – and provide three short examples of how you meet them.

TIP: Put yourself in the employer's shoes and try to think about what they want and need. *Will you help them solve their problems? Are you someone they will enjoy working with? What's in it for them? Consider what you can say – and how – to ensure they will.*

Searching and applying

Have a clear focus on what kind of roles you are searching for. LinkedIn is an excellent place to search; see *page 147 for more information.* Also, try a range of mainstream recruitment consultancies, e.g., Indeed, Reed, and specific sustainability consultants such as Acre (refer to resources at the back of this book*).* Filter your search down to the number of applicants and how long the role has been live so that you apply for jobs you stand the best chance of getting.

Use 'Boolean' to search

A Boolean search is a query technique, via your browser, that utilises Boolean logic to connect individual keywords or phrases within a single query. You use special symbols to define, widen or limit your search to help you find the most relevant results. This includes these key operators: AND, OR, NOT, or NEAR, e.g., ("sustainability" OR "responsible business" OR "ESG") AND ("agriculture" OR "farming"). Run an initial search, then narrow it down into more detail.

Acing your interviews

- Preparation is key, so research the employer to build up your knowledge about them. Check out their website, blog, and social media, including their values and latest news.

- Review the job description again and think of lots of good examples where you can demonstrate how you meet it.

- Practise answers to standard questions and make bullet notes, perhaps using blank flashcards. Find lots of good common interview questions online to research and practise beforehand.

- Other tips include: dress smartly, check the address and directions beforehand, arrive on time, bring a notepad and pen, and prepare a few questions you might ask at the end.

STAR technique

The STAR method is useful for helping you answer interview questions using these four steps: **S**ituation - **T**ask - **A**ction - **R**esult.

Situation: Set the scene and give the context.

Task: Describe your exact role and responsibility.

Action: Provide details about your actions.

Result: Conclude with the result of your action.

STAR is an effective method for interview questions requiring you to demonstrate certain competencies and often start like, '*Give me an example of a time when you...*'

You don't know what the interviewer will ask, but they will normally focus on workplace challenges. This will allow you to demonstrate a range of skills, such as critical thinking, problem-solving, and conflict resolution. As part of your preparation, think about times you have demonstrated these strengths and how that will illustrate how you can excel in this new position.

Three follow-up tips

1. Always follow up after you go for an interview by sending a short thank you email to show your appreciation and enthusiasm.
2. Connect with the interviewers on LinkedIn by sending a connection request with a message. You can then develop a relationship by engaging with their online content.
3. If you feel like the interview went well but aren't offered the job, send an additional email. Thank them and ask for constructive feedback to help you at future interviews.

Exercises

Research and reflect on the following:

1. What jobs excite and motivate you, and how could you learn more about them?

2. Where is there a need in the market, and what could you do to learn more about this?

3. What people, organisations and opportunities might lead you to where you want to be?

4. What are your unique skills and strengths, and in what different ways could you best use them now?

5. What would you do differently to pursue your dream green career now if you had 50 percent more confidence?

Develop your soft skills

It is increasingly recognised that soft skills – non-technical skills which help you succeed in life and work – are also vital for working in sustainability.

Soft skills such as creativity, adaptability, and collaboration are critical in all green jobs.

They are now often referred to as green skills or skills of the future.

Soft skills include personality traits and habits that help you work well with others and achieve your goals. Employers also call them transferable or employability skills.

Due to their importance, we focus on developing these soft skills in our Catalyse Change programme as much as the hard skills for sustainability. In some ways, more, as hard skills can be learned via formal education and online learning, whereas soft skills often need practice and benefit from group learning.

Here are 10 of the top soft skills required by all green occupations:

1. Critical thinking
2. Active listening
3. Reading comprehension
4. Speaking
5. Monitoring
6. Judgement
7. Decision making
8. Complex problem solving
9. Writing
10. Time management

Other essential skills include: adaptability, conflict management, communication, creativity, collaboration, resilience, leadership, positivity, flexibility and teamwork. These skills are complementary to other areas of expertise.

Skills of the future

As new occupations which use artificial intelligence (AI) and digital technologies emerge. Developing your soft or green skills will help you to increase your opportunities and career prospects. These future skills can also help you to; become more adaptable, improve your teamwork skills, and adjust to career changes and new environments. Stay up-to-date with developments and trends by reading the latest reports and data from organisations like Nesta, LinkedIn, and the World Economic Forum. Refer to the resources section at the back of this book for valuable links and ideas.

Exercises

1. **Practice your soft skills**: Think about how you can practice these regularly, e.g.: When you interact with others, take the time to listen to them more attentively, maintain eye contact and be aware of their body language. This will help you to be more empathic and develop better relationships. Or, if you want to improve your communication skills, can you do more writing and public speaking? **Write down 3 things you could try this week.**

2. **Demonstrate your soft skills**: Think of examples in your everyday life – with family, friends, or in lessons – that demonstrate these skills. E.g., where you solved a problem and showed clear communication. **Make some notes below – can you think of 10 good examples?**

3. **Tell these stories**: Write down the examples above and practise telling them interestingly and engagingly. **Create a list of these stories you can use at job interviews to demonstrate your wide-ranging skills.** Practise them alone and through active listening exercises with a friend or accountability buddy.

4. **Write a 'TO DON'T' list**: What do you not want in a new job? E.g., working in an office full time, database/Excel skills. Just because you can do something doesn't mean you should. Use this list to help you understand your skills and interests better, so you can focus on applying for jobs that most interest you and where you will excel.

5. Create a 90-day action plan: Three months – or 90 days – is an effective timescale to plan and manage your time. Try using a simple spreadsheet with your three to five key goals along the top, each with three to five **actions** per week to help you achieve them. **Capture your initial ideas for this here.**

You can receive your own free template of this if you email info@catalysechange.com.

Grow your career with LinkedIn

LinkedIn is essential for job hunting, brand-building, and networking. It now hosts over 900 million members, providing unlimited network connections and job opportunities. Employers use it too. Unlike Instagram, you can build your ideal network using filtered search criteria and you can use it to apply for jobs. However, before you do this, ensure you have a good profile that reflects who you are.

You need a compelling and clear headline and profile when you first start. You must also create consistent content to build your personal and professional brand.

Create a magnetic profile

Be yourself: Your LinkedIn profile is like your website. So, show off a bit about your skills and achievements. This is where a potential employer will look to learn more about you.

Strong profile picture: Ensure you have a professional-looking head and shoulders shot, facing forward, and smiling at the camera.

Headline (directly under your name): Say what you do and what you can do for an employer. Remember, it's not about you, but them. Make it interesting in a way that describes what problem you can solve. Use adjectives to give it energy and flair.

Key skills: Include your relevant key skills, ensuring you have a minimum of five listed. They will appear in any search an employer or recruiter makes.

Don'ts: Avoid using the 'open for work' image frame, saying you are unemployed or 'looking for opportunities'. Companies are looking for someone to help solve their problems. Frame your headline and skills in this way instead.

Open to work: You can tell recruiters you are 'open to work' at the top section of your profile. Only recruiters view it, so your employer won't see it!

About section: Use this to develop your profile. Tell your story. Include your experience, qualifications, skills, achievements, and the opportunities you're seeking. Have a list of roles and skills as 'keywords' at the end, which come up in searches. "Make your profile easier to read by using subheadings and separating the text into small paragraphs. Use emojis to liven it up a little," suggests Sabrina Lee from Impact Agency, who provides a free guide on their website, visit the resources section at the back of this book for the link.

Experience: Detail all your relevant job roles and experience, using a similar format for each one. Include the job title, dates, responsibilities, and results. Be as clear as possible to clarify what you did and achieved.

Recommendations: These will help you build your credibility. You can send requests to people you've previously worked for or with. However, you could also ask other people who can vouch for you, such as teachers, lecturers, or family friends.

Search for jobs

1. **Create job alerts for specific companies**: Go to the company page for a company you would love to work for and follow them. Then select the 'Jobs' tab at the top and set up a job alert.

2. **Let recruiters and employers know you are interested**: Under your 'Settings and privacy,' click 'Data privacy' and then select 'Yes' for 'Signal your interest to recruiters you've created job alerts for' to ensure you get job notifications for companies you like.

3. **Share your profile when you apply**: Under the 'Data privacy' section, select 'Yes' to ensure you share your profile with employers and recruiters.

4. **Share your CV**: There is also a function in 'Job seeking preferences' to change your 'Job application settings' allowing you to upload and share several different CVs depending on the role you're applying for. Give them different titles to tell them apart.

5. **Search and save**: Use the search bar to find jobs and, before you apply, ensure you have listed the right skills to match the job description as closely as possible.

6. **Follow businesses you admire**: Find and follow businesses and organisations you want to work for. This is a great way to learn about them. You can also see who their employees are and perhaps send connection invitations to those whose profiles and roles you are interested in. Develop these relationships to help you better understand the company and be open to future opportunities.

Build your network

1. **Perfect or productive?** Set up your LinkedIn profile so you can start to build your network. Don't worry about it being perfect; you can develop and tweak it as you go.

2. **Make connections**: Connect first with people you know, then people you admire and who work at companies you are interested in. You can also send requests to people connected to your connections. Always send a short note with your connection request, as it is more friendly and makes it more likely that they will respond.

3. **Join the party**: Think of LinkedIn as a party or networking event. Would you thrust a business card into someone's hand and then walk off? Hopefully not! You would probably first introduce yourself and ask them interesting questions. Or join in existing conversations rather than just talk to yourself in the corner!

Create content and engage with people

1. **Add value**. Respond to posts with likes and comments. When commenting, ensure you have read what they have said and respond to it rather than using just a short generic comment. Commenting on existing posts is the way to build relationships and get noticed as other people in their network will also see your comment.

2. **Post your content**. You can repost articles that interest you – always repost with your own comment or summary of it - as well as writing original content through articles and newsletters.

3. **Try the 5x5x5 rule**. To help you start, try liking five posts and adding five comments in five minutes. Sabrina Lee recommends that you, "Try this twice a day for a while, and you will see how much exposure you get in just 10 minutes daily. Remember to like or respond to other people's comments on your content or articles too, as it will help LinkedIn know it's useful and have greater organic reach, meaning more eyes will get on it."

Go for it

- LinkedIn is a great way to build your profile, network, and job prospects.

- Post each day or week and be consistent.

- Don't overthink it, just start regularly posting and chatting and see where it leads. It is not a place to be shy, and it will help you be more confident and visible both on and offline.

- If you are holding back, see what thoughts come up for you, and use the exercises on page 80 to help you reframe them.

- It is free and a great tool for finding and growing your green career – so give it a go and just get started.

Exercises

1. Find five organisations or businesses on LinkedIn that interest you. Write them down here and describe what you like about each of them.

2. **Find five people you admire** who work in sustainability. What inspires you about them? Find ways to connect with these people or organisations and stay in touch. Add at least ten new contacts each day or week for a month.

3. **Follow three businesses and organisations** you love and create a job alert for each one. You could build on this by following three new ones each week or month.

4. **Imagine attending a networking meeting** in your local city or town. Or better still, go to a real one! How does doing it make you feel? What helps you to do it? What holds you back from going or from feeling comfortable when you are there? What one action could help you? Can you turn it into a regular action for your 90-day planner? E.g., go to one networking meeting a week or month. Perhaps ask a friend or your accountability buddy to go with you?

5. **Create your dream job**: Dayna Isom Johnson is Etsy's resident trend expert – a job that didn't exist until she created it. She identified what she loved to do and asked Etsy's leadership to create a role that fitted her talent and excitement. What would your dream job be? How can you research it? How could you approach an existing business or charity about whether they need a role like this? It's brave, bold, and different, but why not? Perhaps you need to be further down your career journey or already be working for a business before you do this. But it's worth thinking about now.

Catalyst top tips

Eilish and Olivia share tips for pursuing your dream green career.

Eilish used a gap year for work experience before starting a biology degree at Oxford University.

"1. **Do what you love and what you are good at**. They are usually the same thing – this will give you a reason to go to work and give you the power you need to make an impact. If you genuinely love what you are doing, you will be a force for good. Then you can find a way to impact the planet with your chosen career positively.

2. **Get experience**. Education is essential, but from what I have heard, experience is something that employers look for the most. The more experience you have, the more employable you are, and you are more likely to get that job you want. I gained experience working with the London Wildlife Trust by emailing them. Only some people will reply, but

the more people you ask, the more likely someone will say yes!

3. Say yes to everything! It has been a rule of mine in life to take up every opportunity. There are times to say no, but when it comes to jobs, experience, things to bulk up your CV, or that have a positive impact on the planet, you can never do enough!

People do often like to help, and so it is always worth asking, as the worst that can happen is that they say no. I got to learn about the illegal wildlife trade directly by speaking with E.J Milner Gulland who founded the Saiga Conservation Alliance, and would not have gotten this opportunity if I had not asked!

In the summer, I went to an island called Tom Owens Caye in Placencia, Belize, and learned how to dive working with Reef Conservation International. This was an incredible experience – so my advice would be to do scary things, because it was quite intimidating doing this on my own, but one of the best experiences! I hope to do something similar this summer.

Also go to as many free events as you can, as it will give you a feeling for what you are most passionate about, and might help you decide the direction of your green career."

Eilish Farrelly, student

Olivia is an environmental consultant and radio presenter who lives in Bristol. She has a degree and a master's in chemical engineering from the University of Edinburgh.

"1. **Your future job may not have even been created yet!** So don't get hung up on the job title. Equip yourself with skills and knowledge around what you are passionate about, and be bold in taking opportunities outside your comfort zone.

2. **Sustainability and 'green' are in every part of life**. So, work with different people and teams and take a multi-disciplinary approach to get comfortable with that.

3. **Don't worry if your job isn't 'green'.** Any job can be green if you help make the company or the people act more sustainably. So, if you have a part-time job

while studying, see what you can learn about their sustainability plans/responsibilities and help to improve them."

Olivia Sweeney, Environmental Consultant

Other useful tips

To stay relevant in the sustainability job market, staying up to date with the latest skills, developments, and trends is crucial. Here are a few tips to help you:

Take online courses:

Many free online courses can help you grow your green knowledge and skills. While more advanced paid courses can also help you stay current with the latest concepts, tools, and frameworks.

Attend conferences and webinars:

These are a great way to learn about emerging themes and related issues. Many of these events are free or low-cost and can now be easily accessed online.

Join professional organisations:

Joining professional organisations can provide you with access to a community of professionals working in this field. They often offer networking opportunities, training, and resources to help you stay up to date with the latest trends and developments.

Read industry publications:

Several industry publications cover sustainability and environment, social and governance (ESG) topics. They often provide insights and analysis on the latest developments in the field. Register to their mailing lists and read them regularly to stay up to date.

See the resources section at the back for ideas.

SECTION 4:

BUILDING YOUR COMMUNITY

Building your community

You cannot do anything of real impact on your own. Nothing of value can be achieved in isolation. You must work in collaboration with other like-minded people and partners. So, take time to nurture good connections and build your community. What does this look like, and how could you go about it?

"If you want to go quickly, go alone. If you want to go far, go together." **African Proverb**

If you want to make change happen, you need to find other people who are also interested in doing the same thing. You cannot do it alone.

How I built my community

When I moved back to Bristol in 2015, I started to explore how I could help young women to make a difference.

I had just started working for myself as a consultant, supporting social enterprises and charities to be sustainable through delivering projects, coaching, and workshops.

I'd been away from Bristol for 10 years living and working in Cornwall and Devon, so I didn't have many current contacts there.

However, Bristol's year as European Green Capital had just started, so it was a great time to arrive and work in sustainability. I met lots of great people through the many events taking place.

Also, I asked my old colleagues at the Soil Association for some introductions and referrals.

This was pre-pandemic when people usually met in person rather than online. So, we would meet in a cafe to get to know each other and explore collaboration. I would learn about them and tell them about my new business as a consultant in sustainability and social enterprise.

However, when I started to talk about my real passion – women's empowerment – the energy seemed to shift. I got such a positive reaction. Everyone saw the need to help empower young women. Even though many women already work in sustainability, there are significant gaps in STEM sectors and leadership positions. Gaps also develop in many girls' confidence as the teenage years progress.

We explored how to create a safe space to connect young women with like-minded peers and mentors. Women already working in the climate and social impact space, to guide and support them as role models and advocates, to help amplify their potential and progress.

This is how Catalyse Change was born.

But it may never have happened if I hadn't received help from all these supportive, innovative, and knowledgeable people early on.

- Three of the women I spoke to: Jenna Holliday, Julie Ellison, and Rhian Sherrington, joined me to form our first Board of Directors.

- Local umbrella organisation Bristol Green Capital Partnership helped us to launch. This is also where we met our first Advisory Board members: Gemma Perkins, Heloise Balme, Jennifer Best, Jessica Ferrow, Kate Bruintjes, Sara Telahoun, and Amelia Twine.

- Lots of other brilliant women and businesses also helped us launch by supporting our Crowdfunder and our first-ever Catalyst Bootcamp at Bristol University in 2016.

The lesson here is that you can't do anything in isolation. You've got to find your tribe.

"A tribe is a group of people connected to one another, connected to a leader, and connected to an idea. For millions of years, human beings have been part of one tribe or another. A group needs only two things to be a tribe: a shared interest and a way to communicate." **Seth Godin, author, entrepreneur, and teacher**

We've already explored how to define your purpose, grow your confidence, build your resilience, and develop the skills you need for getting a job. However, building your network or community is just as important. Did you know that geese which fly in formation fly 70 percent further and faster?

Here are a few ideas to help you get started right now.

Exercises

1. **Talk to people**. You never know who you're going to meet next. Attend a local event on a topic you are interested in. Join a like-minded group, a climate cafe or club! Discuss your interests with people you meet – you don't know who might be listening. Just talking to people can spark incredible opportunities. Jot down some ideas for some of the people and places you would like to connect with and research further.

2. **Get networking**. There are now so many different opportunities to network and meet like-minded people. Whether it's green mingles, climate-action training, or political meetings. Check them out and go in person if you can. However, plenty are online, too – so there is no excuse not to get involved!

3. **Use social media**. Follow people you like and engage with them. Also, post about the things you're interested in and share your thoughts. What are you most passionate about? What do you want to be known for? Who are you interested in meeting? These are the sorts of things that you want to talk about. Use hashtags that interest you. Tag people you want to connect with. You can build a solid and engaged network by being active and strategic online. Check out the resources section at the back of this book for contacts and ideas.

The power of mentoring

At Catalyse Change, we inspire and empower young women and non-binary changemakers. One of the ways we do this is by connecting them with a mentor and network of professional female role models. But what is mentoring, and why is it a good idea to help develop your green career?

"A mentor is someone who sees more talent and ability within you than you see in yourself and helps bring it out of you."
Bob Proctor, self-help author & lecturer

Our mentors provide one-to-one support to young women helping them identify and achieve a goal related to pursuing a career in sustainability.

- **A mentor is** a trusted and experienced advisor who gives a less experienced person hope, encouragement, and practical advice.

- **A mentor is not** a therapist, counsellor, or coach, a cure-all, nor a one-way street.

A mentor helps you:

- Understand your potential career opportunities and the pathways to achieving them.

- Clarify your goals and be held accountable for them.

- Sharpen your CV or interviewing technique.

- Build your confidence and support you into your next life stage.

It is a powerful way to help you learn about yourself and help you achieve your goals.

Sara Telahoun, a climate consultant supporting local authorities in taking climate action and who has been a Catalyse Change mentor for a few years, says: "I am a mentor because now more than ever, young people – especially those who don't see themselves represented – need support in building their confidence and self-belief to have satisfying, impactful careers. As a mentor, I've learnt so much from these young women: to bring positive energy, compassion and innovative solutions to global issues. I recommend mentoring through Catalyse Change to any other sustainability professional interested in growing their skills, supporting others, and inspiring the next generation of changemakers."

Zoe Montgomery, a Catalyse Change alumni, shares the benefits of having a mentor:

"I graduated with a master's in sustainable development and was trying to figure out what to do with my life. The comprehensive course allowed me to explore various elements of sustainable development, including consumption patterns, behaviour change, and policy on a local and national level. I am drawn towards food systems as they encompass many global challenges, from the obvious, like health and well-being, to gender equality, climate change, animal rights, and biodiversity loss. I've struggled and felt under pressure to find my 'purpose', i.e., a job that creates positive change, and have the confidence in my skills to go for opportunities. So, the mentoring programme appealed to me as I wanted to develop my confidence and gain a bit of direction for future career possibilities."

Zoe shares some of her learning and tips here:
What did it involve?

- I met with my mentor monthly over video call for about an hour. During this time, we reflected on the actions I set myself the previous month and what habits or practices had helped me.

- My mentor then provided resources to explore further ideas we discussed, such as videos, articles, or activities.

- Reflection has been a big part of the mentoring, which I struggled with initially. I now have a daily gratitude practice and try to dedicate time to focus on a particular skill I'd like to develop, or a habit I want to implement.

What were the benefits?

- I have gained more clarity on the industry I want to work in, and I've become more confident in talking about my key skills.

- I didn't used to talk about career options, goal setting, or skills development, as other people couldn't relate to my situation. Now, I have a dedicated person to discuss these things with, allowing me to explore and research topics I might otherwise not have thought to explore.

- My mentor greatly supported me, providing accountability and advice beyond my career path. Having someone more experienced to talk with about my worries and progress provided a new perspective and pushed me to identify my goals, values, and strengths.

Tips for getting the most out of a mentorship

- **View it as a relationship.** Don't view your mentor as someone who can solve all your problems – they are there to help, of course, but also to learn!

- **Start with a mindset of 'what you put in, you'll get out'.** You're only going to get out as much as the effort you put in.

- **Take it step by step**. Things won't change overnight, but you will start to see a difference with intentional practices.

"I define connection as the energy between people when they feel seen, heard, and valued; when they can give and receive without judgement, and when they derive sustenance and strength from the relationship." **Brené Brown, storyteller & researcher**

Exercises

1. **Reflective practice**: Build this into your day or week to help you understand what is working well, what you find challenging, and where you might need support. Use your journal to help you explore and remember your insights. **Capture any initial thoughts about it here now**.

2. **Research opportunities**: Find out more about what mentoring involves (see the resources at the back of the book) to explore whether you would like to try it. Contact Catalyse Change about their mentoring programme info@catalysechange.com. **What could be your top 5 actions to help you progress this?**

Activism: taking action

Activism helps create change on behalf of a cause. It can be an effective way to make a difference – fast. Fridays for Future, the global youth-led climate movement, was a game changer. Sparking a global awakening for climate action, putting pressure on policymakers, and bringing changemakers together. What are the different ways you can engage in activism? How do you keep yourself safe and avoid burnout?

"I raise my voice, not so that I can shout,
But so that those without a voice can be heard."
Malala Yousafzai, Pakistani Activist and Nobel Peace Prize winner

From Joan of Arc to Greta Thunberg, girls and women have always led resistance movements. This is because we understand inequality as we experience it every day. However, we don't need great people to lead us. We need to join like-minded communities and just get on with it.

In her brilliant book *It's Not That Radical*, Mikaela Loach, author and climate activist, says, "We absolutely cannot afford to wait. We cannot afford to rely on anyone else to save us. We have to realise that the future has to be ours to change ourselves."

Getting started

Grassroots activism comes from people just like you and me. It builds movements for change by bringing people together to raise their voices against those with more power. Organisations such as Amnesty International and Plan UK, have campaigning information and toolkits on their websites. Also, check out Kaelyn Rich's book *Girls Resist!* for ideas on how to start a campaign. You can find these links in the resources section at the back of this book.

Join an existing movement

You can get involved in climate and social sustainability activism in lots of ways. So many organisations are already doing brilliant work, so why not join them? Do some online research to see who is out there. To learn more and find out how to support them, sign up for their mailing lists and follow them on socials e.g.,

- **Campaigning**: Avaaz, City to Sea, Extinction Rebellion (XR).

- **Environmental**: Friends of the Earth, Greenpeace, Sierra Club, Woodland Trust.

- **Local**: Check out the notice boards in your school, university, library, independent cafe, or whole foods shop. Stay informed by signing up for their newsletters.

Issues to consider

- **Intersectionality**: We are all part of different social categories, e.g., gender, social class, racialisation, (dis)ability, which intersect, providing overlapping forms of discrimination and marginalisation. To act with or on behalf of other people, we must examine how their experiences and identities intersect with ours. Also, consider your structural privilege and how that might make your actions oppressive or exclusionary to others. Acting with intersectionality means acting with awareness of privilege to create equality.

- **Legal**: While the right to protest in the UK is legal, there are things you need to be aware of before organising or participating in one. The European Convention on Human Rights currently protects the right to protest. However, this only applies to peaceful protest and does not extend to any violence inflicted or damage caused. This right is not absolute and can be limited in certain circumstances. The UK government is trying to erode these freedoms, so stay informed and up to date before taking action.

- **Safety and avoiding burnout**: Self-care is essential for resilient activism. Explore and develop techniques for protecting your safety and well-being. Learn tools to help you best focus your energy and activities. See the chapter on Building your Resilience.

Feeling stuck? Here are a few ideas to help you.

Exercises

1. **Create a mind map**: Kaelyn Rich suggests mind-mapping your thoughts and ideas. Start with a central circle on a blank piece of paper. Write or draw a topic or image meaningful to you around taking action. Then draw other circles around it with causes and issues you care about. Around each circle, draw lines coming out of it. Write why you care about that issue and what you would do if money were no object. Write down everything you can think of. Then see which of the circles has the most lines around them. Is this the one you feel most passionately about? Then make this the number one issue to focus on. Either start your campaign around this or join an existing one.

Draw your mind map here:

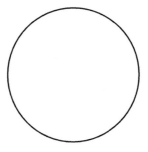

2. **Watch this**: It's normal to feel anxious or overwhelmed by climate change, says psychologist Renée Lertzman. Can we turn those feelings into something productive? In her TED talk, she discusses the emotional effects of climate change and offers insights on how psychology can help us, by discovering the creativity and resilience needed to act. Watch her TED Talk – How to Turn Climate Anxiety into Action. **What comes up for you when you watch this?**

3. **Support a political party**: Volunteer for a local party you want to help. From distributing leaflets to joining a phone bank. It's a great way to make a difference while learning new skills and meeting new like-minded local people. **Research your local options.**

4. **Join inspirational groups**: Sign up to their mailing lists to receive updates about their campaigns, workshops, and events so you can stay current, support, and join wherever possible. See the resources section at the end of this book for more information. **Who would you like to find out more about and what are your next steps?**

5. **Know your carbon footprint**: Do you know your carbon footprint? Use one of the tools listed in the resources section, such as Giki Zero or WWF. It is a valuable process to help you think about how you can live out your values more fully. What one significant change can you make to your life now to affect your carbon footprint? Try it for a month and see how you feel. **Use your journal to explore any impacts it has on your life.**

"If political leaders don't act with greater ambition now, our kids and grandkids will look back at this moment with such anger and bewilderment. How on earth could it be, knowing what we know, we didn't act faster when we still had time?"

Caroline Lucas, Green MP

SECTION 5:

CHOOSING YOUR FUTURE

Choosing your future

We can't be held responsible for the decisions and behaviour of other people. However, we can live out our values by who we choose to be now. We create our present and future with our thoughts, words, and actions, which generate multiple ripple effects, often in ways we can't begin to understand. What future are you choosing? How are you showing up? Is it as the person you want to be now?

"People forget what you say, but not how you make them feel."
Maya Angelou

I was an angry activist when I was young, often ranting about climate change, inequality, and capitalism, yet mostly with little impact.

People respond best to what makes them feel good – not to being told off or made to feel stupid or scared.

Think about the people you admire most. The people who bring joy into your life.

Perhaps your family members or your friends. Maybe a climate leader or film star?

- What is it that you love about them?
- Is it because they make you feel good in some way?
- Do they demonstrate the things you admire?
- Is it because they're authentic, confident, and courageous?
- Perhaps it's because they're funny, creative, and bold.

Think about who **you** are talking to and what you want **them** to feel. Think about the impact your words and actions might be having on them. People respond best to joy, love, connection, and how we make them feel.

Use your intuition

A deep well of wisdom is available to us whenever we need it. But it takes practise to learn the language of intuition.

When you connect with this inner wisdom, you'll gain the clarity you need to trust its guidance. It will help you access flow and synchronicity for your changemaker journey. This will enable your confidence and courage to grow.

A good way to access your intuition is to ask this question and listen for your instinctive answer:

"If I believed all of life is organising around my success, what would I do in this situation? What would my decision be?"

If something isn't working for you, look at the deep knowing you already have inside you. Are you listening to it? Are you acting on it? If not, is this because you are afraid or just not taking the time to listen? You need to trust your inner wisdom and develop a practice to help you access it.

Find your changemaker superpower

Be confident to express your authentic self. Share the unique gifts you bring.

Stop being scared when you are in your zone of authenticity. That is when you shine.

That is when you inspire others. That is when life flows and is joyful.

I invite you to find and share your changemaker

superpower.

Exercises

1. **What's your changemaker superpower?** Think about three things in your life that feel effortless to you but which others find more challenging. Also, think of something you have done that has amazed other people. Then think of a time in your life you have felt fearless; describe what you did and how it felt. **Write your reflections and see if your unique superpowers are revealed to you.** *Many thanks to Jessica Ferrow who used this at a Catalyse Change workshop.*

2. **Write a letter from the future**. Take some quiet time to visualise yourself and your life five years from now. Then write yourself a letter from your future self who is already living the life you want. Get into free flow and explore the following. What are you doing? Where do you live? What excites you? What lessons do you want to pass on to your younger self? You will see what is most important to you when you read this back. **Keep it to help you set goals and actions for yourself.**

3. **Access your intuition**. I love this exercise from
Claire Zammit. Ask yourself: What would my
decision be if I believed all of life is organising around
my success? Even though you might not have any
evidence for it, and even if you're not sure you believe
it. Just for a moment, act as if it is. And instead of
thinking about the answer, let your awareness drop
down into your body and move into a place of
listening. Notice any sounds, sensations, feelings,
visuals, or even colours. **Write down what comes
up for you.**

4. **Shift your limiting beliefs**. A limiting paradigm is a way of seeing and thinking about yourself. To shift this, Jinny Ditzler, author of *Your Best Year Yet*, says you must ask yourself the following two questions and journal your answers: In what areas of my life am I not achieving what I want? What do I say to myself to explain these failures? Circle the answers with the strongest influence on you, which you consider to be the truth. Now think about what is holding this limiting belief in place. Create a new empowering belief or paradigm about it instead. **Practice transforming your thinking to the new paradigm every time you slip into the old one.**

5. **Your perfect day**. Rather than thinking about long-term plans, Megan Fraser, climate coach, suggests just focusing on what one perfect day looks like for you. What are the core elements of your perfect day? Identify the building blocks that are present in a perfect 24-hour period. Use these guiding questions to help you: When I feel satisfaction and pride at the end of the day, what created that feeling? What actions did I take? What traps did I avoid? **Journal on your reflections.**

Women in leadership

Leadership can be unappealing to many women. Women leaders often have to act like men to succeed. Women are leaving leadership roles in large numbers and burnout is at an all-time high. While women in public life – from politicians to actors – appear to receive harsher treatment and judgement than their male counterparts. What does leadership mean to you? Do you need to be a leader to succeed in your dream green career?

"To solve our beautiful, bright planet's dark problems, we must refuse to be ruled by fear. We must discard the belief that we're powerless, and realise that we are infinitely powerful."
Clover Hogan, climate activist

Leadership is not for the few but for the many. We need LOTS of brilliant and compassionate leaders. However, leadership looks different for many people and can take various forms.

Only some people want to be a CEO, but inspiring a team or managing a project is still leadership. It is about defining what is suitable for you. This climate emergency demands action. Everyone needs to be inspired and engaged to help solve it. So, find ways to lead change through whichever vehicle is best for you.

What does leadership look like to me? In some ways, I'm a natural leader. I've spoken out publicly on issues that matter to me. I've organised and led events and protests. I managed teams of people and projects during my 18-year career at the Soil Association.

Also, I'm not a leader. I'm not comfortable with conflict and complex negotiations. I don't like long meetings. I don't really enjoy developing strategies and policies. I'm more of a doer. I like to lead by example.

Work to your strengths. You need to understand your personality and strengths. Know what you enjoy and what you are most comfortable with. I've encountered work situations where I haven't wanted to take a central stage, but felt embarrassed about admitting that.

Do you have to be a leader? Working in climate action and sustainability, you can feel obliged to speak up at every chance. During my career, I have spoken on TV and local radio and written articles for printed media. But it's not a place I sit comfortably, or I have wanted to pursue actively. Sometimes that has made me feel like I'm not good enough or that I need to do more to prove myself. However, leadership can take many different forms.

Do what you enjoy. You don't have to be on a political stage to be a leader. You don't have to run a podcast or do TV interviews if you don't want to. Find out what you enjoy and are most comfortable with.

Leadership takes many forms

- Are you vegan or vegetarian because of your ethics?
- Do you cycle and use public transport because of the environment?
- Do you treat everyone respectfully because you believe in equality?

These acts are all forms of leadership.

You are acting according to your values and are a

role model to others. You don't have to talk on a public platform if that's not where your skills or motivations lie.

There are many different types of leaders. Which does leadership mean to you?

"Do what you feel in your heart to be right – for you'll be criticised anyway."

Eleanor Roosevelt, the former First Lady of the US

Do you have imposter syndrome?

Yes, the system does need to change. However, the most significant thing holding many of us back is ourselves. Imposter syndrome is a phrase that describes a feeling of not being good enough for your role. It is a surprisingly common experience – especially for women – and can seriously undermine your confidence. It is the feeling that your achievements are not genuine or that you do not deserve praise or success.

People with imposter syndrome believe they have hidden their incompetence and will soon be 'found out'. It is a powerful and derailing experience that can leave you feeling alone and ashamed.

I felt like an imposter for a long time in my career, as I didn't have a degree. I had chosen to travel and work overseas for over five years instead of attending university. However, when I started working for the Soil Association, I was quickly promoted from an entry-level admin role to a manager. I was proactive and liked finding solutions to the challenges of a rapidly growing charity and social business.

During my career there, I managed many teams of people and a £2 million project. You don't get those opportunities unless you do a good job and people believe in you. Yet I still felt inadequate. So, unfortunately, I spent many years not fully allowing myself to enjoy my success and fulfil my potential. I thought the only way to prove my worth was to work harder. While I should have probably focused more of my efforts on strategy, networking, and personal development.

Imposter syndrome is widespread, especially for women. A good place to start addressing it is by acknowledging your feelings and talking to a trusted friend or mentor about them.

We don't have time to do the whole subject justice here, but there is a lot of great advice out there to help you. If this subject resonates with you, check out the TED talk from Elizabeth Cox, *What is imposter syndrome and how can you combat it?* You can find this in the resources section at the end of this book.

Exercises

1. **Women you admire**: Think about five women you admire. Write down their names on one line, and underneath each one write five words that describe what you admire, e.g., bravery, intelligence, humour etc. When you have finished, read the words, and see which three stand out the most.

2. **Is this you too?** Once you have decided on the three top qualities above, cover up the names at the top of the paper, and read back the words putting 'I am' before each of them, e.g., I am brave, honest, courageous etc. We can usually see qualities in other people which we value the most. However, it is often hard to see them in ourselves. How does this feel? **Capture how this feels for you.**

3. **Ask a friend**: Another good way to do this is by asking friends or family members who know you well to tell you what they believe to be your top three qualities. **Accept these compliments graciously and make a note of what comes up for you when you hear them.**

4. **What does leadership look like for you?** Take some time to think about leadership and what's important to you. Find somewhere quiet where you won't be interrupted for at least 10 minutes and use the following prompts to guide your thinking. **Write down what comes up for you when you do this.**

What qualities feel essential to you in a leader and for you to be a leader? What does good leadership look like in others and yourself? What does good leadership feel like? What does a good leader think about?

5. **Your sustainability blueprint**: To help you better understand yourself and your next steps, answer the following questions, drawing from your learning in this book. *What is; my visionary 'what if' question or the problem I want to solve? What am I good at and love doing? What is my top confidence tip or trick? What sustainability sector/s am I most drawn to? What would be my preferred job role/s?* Reflect on what you have written and how it can help you direct your green career journey. This is something you can come back to and develop over time.

_____

_____

_____

_____

_____

_____

_____

_____

_____

_____

_____

_____

_____

Enjoy the journey

I hope this book has interested and inspired you – your changemaker journey should be exciting. However, it's not always easy, and it is brave of you to come so far. Opening yourself up to new possibilities and challenging yourself can be scary. So, I want you to know you are already doing a great job, and I am proud of you. Here are some final exercises to help you reflect on where you are now.

1. **What does your dream career and life look like?** Imagine what it looks like for you. Where do you work? Who are you serving? What problems are you solving? What does your dream life look and feel like? Use creative visualisation to imagine this and capture your ideas.

2. **How does your career journey make you feel?**
   Take some time to explore where you are currently
   at with this. Journal your reflections.

3. **What inspires you?** Think of a time you felt
   inspired. To help you, close your eyes and place
   your hand on your heart – it's a valuable way to
   connect to how it feels like for you.

4. **What would be different if you thought of your
   changemaker journey like this?** Reflect on this
   question again. Ask yourself, 'What would I do if I

had 50 percent more confidence?' Journal your
reflections.

_____

_____

_____

_____

_____

5. **What have you learned from this book**? At
   Catalyse Change, we end our sessions with time to
   reflect and consider the next steps. Also, to share
   something we are grateful for, which helps us
   connect with our hearts rather than our heads. It
   also reduces stress and increases well-being,
   making it a great way to end any meeting, event, or
   day.

_____

_____

_____

_____

Take a few minutes to write down the following final reflections:

- What is your top takeaway from this book?
- What is one new thing you have learned?
- What one action will you do this week?
- What three things are you most grateful for today?

Celebrate and learn from your journey as you go.

Use reflection and journaling as an ongoing practice to help you.

Start a weekly routine of reflecting on what you have learned that week.

What have I done well? What worked, and what can I celebrate? What am I most proud of? How does it feel? How can I use it to learn and develop my skills?

Good luck and remember to walk with others who are on a similar journey.

Resources & websites to help you

Green jobs and skills

Aldersgate group, Skills for a New Economy
www.aldersgategroup.org.uk/

British Council, Green Careers Directory
www.britishcouncil.org/

Catalyse Change, Green Education Guide
https://mailchi.mp/catalysechange/green-education-report

Edie.net www.edie.net/

EAUC, Sustainability Careers Guide
www.eauc.org.uk/sustainability_careers_guide

EAUC, Sustainability Exchange
www.sustainabilityexchange.ac.uk/careers1

IEMA, Green Careers

Hub www.greencareershub.com/about/

LinkedIn, Global Green Skills Report
https://economicgraph.linkedin.com/en-us/research/global-green-skills-report

Nesta, Innovation Agency for Social Good
www.nesta.org.uk/sustainable-future/

PwC, Green Jobs Barometer www.pwc.co.uk

Students Organising For Sustainability www.sos-uk.org/

My World of Work www.myworldofwork.co.uk/

Groundwork, Green Careers

www.groundwork.org.uk/growing-green-careers-report/

Online learning

Coursera www.coursera.org/

Ecodemy https://ecodemy.ca/

Free Courses for Jobs https://skillsforlife.campaign.gov.uk

Future Learn www.futurelearn.com/

LinkedIn https://linkedin.com/learning

Massive Open Online Courses (MOOCs)

www.mooc.org/

National Careers Service

https://nationalcareers.service.gov.uk/

Open University www.open.ac.uk/

The Skills Network https://theskillsnetwork.com/

Getting a job

Specialist sustainability recruitment

Allen and Yorke www.allen-york.com/

Acre www.acre.com/

Charity Jobs www.charityjob.co.uk/

Climate 17 www.climate17.com/

Conservation Jobs https://www.conservation-careers.com/

Countryside Jobs www.countrysidejobslink.co.uk/

Countryside Jobs Service www.countryside-jobs.com/

Environment Job www.environmentjob.co.uk/

Environment Jobs www.environmentjobs.co.uk/

Environmental Science www.environmentalscience.org/

Evergreen Resources https://evergreen.org.uk/

Green Choices www.greenchoices.org/

Green Jobs www.greenjobs.co.uk/

Greenworx www.greenworkx.org/

Lantra www.lantra.co.uk/

Terra.do https://terra.do/

The Guardian https://jobs.theguardian.com/jobs

Third Sector Jobs https://jobs.thirdsector.co.uk/

TPP Not for Profit www.tpp.co.uk/

Graduate career websites

AAI Employability www.aai-employability.org.uk/

Change Agents UK www.changeagents.org.uk/

Jobs Graduate www.jobs-graduate.co.uk/

Milk Round www.milkround.com/

Prospects www.prospects.ac.uk/

Scot Grad www.ourskillsforce.co.uk/

Target Jobs https://targetjobs.co.uk/

Mainstream recruitment

Indeed https://uk.indeed.com/

Monster www.monster.co.uk/

Reed www.reed.co.uk/

Simply Hired www.simplyhired.co.uk/

Other pathways

Social Enterprise

Prince's Trust www.princes-trust.org.uk/

School for Social Entrepreneurs www.the-sse.org/

Apprenticeships

IfATE www.instituteforapprenticeships.org/

UK

England www.apprenticeships.gov.uk/

Scotland www.apprenticeships.scot/

Wales www.gov.wales/

Northern Ireland www.nidirect.gov.uk/

Other useful support

Big Issue Recruit https://jobs.bigissue.com/

Careers Box www.careersbox.co.uk/

Squiggly Careers (podcasts) www.amazingif.com/listen/

Coaching

Climate Change Coaches

https://climatechangecoaches.com/

Rhian Sherrington, Transitions Coach

https://womeninsustainability.net

Traci Lewis, Green Career Coach

https://tracilewis.co.uk/

Mentoring

Catalyse Change https://catalysechange.com/

Girls' Network www.thegirlsnetwork.org.uk/

Girls Out Loud https://girlsoutloud.org.uk/

STEMETTES https://stemettes.org/

Campaigns and communities

Avaaz https://secure.avaaz.org/

CIWEM, Pass the mic climate www.ciwem.org/

Climate Cardinals www.climatecardinals.org/

Friends of the Earth https://friendsoftheearth.uk/

Greenpeace www.greenpeace.org.uk/

Letters to the Earth https://www.letterstotheearth.com/

People and Planet

https://peopleandplanet.org/about/about-us

Plan UK https://plan-uk.org/act-for-girls/act-for-girls-toolkit

Stop Ecocide International www.stopecocide.earth/

Voting Counts https://votingcounts.org.uk/

 XR https://extinctionrebellion.uk/

350.org https://350.org/

Youth Organisations

Black to Nature https://black2nature.org/

Black Geographers www.blackgeographers.com/

Black Girls Hike www.bghuk.com/

Catalyse Change CIC https://catalysechange.com

Force of Nature www.forceofnature.xyz/ (eco-anxiety support)

Girl Guiding, Generation Green www.girlguiding.org.uk/

Resilience Project www.theresilienceproject.org.uk (eco-anxiety support)

Youth Do It www.youthdoit.org/

Well-being & mental health support

Climate Mental Health Network

www.climatementalhealth.net/

NHS www.nhs.uk/every-mind-matters/mental-wellbeing-tips/youth-mental-health/

Mind www.mind.org.uk/

Samaritans www.samaritans.org/

Young Minds www.youngminds.org.uk/

Mindfulness apps

Calm www.calm.com/

Headspace www.headspace.com/

Insight Timer https://insighttimer.com/

Carbon Footprint tools

Climate Hero https://carbon-calculator.climatehero.me/

Giki zero https://zero.giki.earth/

WWF https://footprint.wwf.org.uk/

Recommended reading & listening

My top 5 climate books

1. Climate Justice, Mary Robinson
2. It's Not That Radical, Mikaela Loach
3. The Climate Book, Greta Thunberg
4. This Changes Everything, Naomi Klein
5. Why Women Will Save The Planet, Friends of the Earth

Books to help you take action

1. Manifesto: The Battle For Green Britain, Dale Vince
2. The Solutionists, Solitaire Townsend
3. Do Good, Get Paid, Natalie Fee
4. Project Drawdown, Paul Hawken
5. The Carbon Almanac, Seth Godin

Eco-anxiety (books)

1. A Guide To Eco-anxiety, Anouchka Grose
2. It's Not Just You, Tori Tsui
3. A Field Guide To Eco-anxiety, Sarah Jacquette Ray

4. Sacred Instructions, Sherri Mitchell

5. Turn The Tide On Climate Anxiety, Megan Kennedy-Woodward, Dr Patrick Kennedy-Wiliams

Eco-anxiety (podcasts)

1. Force of Nature, Clover Hogan

2. How to Save a Planet, Dr Ayana Elzabeth Johnson and Alex Bumberg

3. Outrage + Optimism, Christiana Figueres, Tom Rivet-Carnac and Paul Dickinson

4. The Yikes Podcast, Mikaela Loach and Jo Becker

5. From What If to What Next, Rob Hopkins

TED Talks www.ted.com/talks

1. Start with why, Simon Sinek

2. Power of vulnerability, Brené Brown

3. A healthy economy should be designed to thrive not grow, Kate Raworth

4. What to do when climate change feels unstoppable, Clover Hogan

5. Sustainability topics

www.ted.com/topics/sustainability

Inspiring books

1. Active Hope, Joanna Macy & Chris Johnstone
2. Dare To Be Great, Polly Higgins
3. The Transition Handbook, Rob Hopkins
4. Saving Us, Katharine Hayhoe
5. The Future We Choose, Christiana Figueres & Tom Rivett-Carnac.

Personal development books

1. The Success Principles, Jack Canfield
2. Your Best Year Yet, Jinny Ditzler
3. Mindset, Carol Dweck
4. Reframe Your Story, Tammy Heerman
5. The Four Agreements, Don Miguel Ruiz

These resources will help you on your changemaker journey. It isn't a comprehensive list, but it includes some people and books that have inspired me. They will, in turn, provide you with new ideas and signpost you to others who will direct you further.

References

P1   Green Taskforce Report to Government Industry and Skills
        Sector
        www.gov.uk/government/publications/green-jobs-
        taskforce-report
        United Nations
        www.un.org/en/academic-impact/sustainability

P2   Climate Justice www.friendsoftheearth.uk

P3   Equality vs equity www.risetowin.org

P8   Does Gender Diversity in the workplace mitigate climate
        change? Science Direct
        www.sciencedirect.com/
        Why investing in women is vital for sustainability, OMFIF
        www.omfif.org/
        Research: Women are better leaders during a crisis, Harvard
        Business Review (HBR)
        https://hbr.org/

P9   Gender pay gap in the UK: 2022, Office National Statistics
        www.ons.gov.uk
        Why everyone should prioritise gender equality in leadership,
        IBM
        www.ibm.com/
        Lack of confidence isn't what's holding women back, Atlantic
        www.theatlantic.com
        The Authority Gap, Mary Ann Sieghart
        https://guardianbookshop.com/the-authority-gap-
        9780857527561

P10   Non-Binary, Teen Vogue
        www.teenvogue.com/tag/non-binary

P11   Catalyse Change CIC www.catalysechange.com

Gender Equality at Every Stage: a roadmap for change, UK government www.gov.uk/

Act for Girls Rights, Plan UK: https://plan-uk.org/

P12 Youth Advisory Group on Climate Change, UN www.un.org/en/climatechange

This Changes Everything, Naomi Klein https://naomiklein.org/this-changes-everything/

Research: Women are better leaders during a crisis, Harvard Business Review https://hbr.org

Why investing in women is key for a green future, Barbara Rambousek, OMFIF https://www.omfif.org/

BLOG: Gender equality in leadership, IBM https://www.ibm.com/blogs/nordic-msp/why-everyone-should-prioritize-gender-equality-in-leadership/

P13 Africa Report, CDP www.cdp.net

Climate change: Focus on girls and young women, Plan International https://plan-international.org/

Women must be protagonists in solving the climate crisis, Amazon Watch https://amazonwatch.org

Women's Rights, Amnesty International www.amnesty.org

P14 Climate Justice, Mary Robinson www.mrfcj.org/

P15 Anita Roddick https://en.wikipedia.org/wiki/Anita_Roddick

Permaculture www.permaculture.org.uk/

P21 Energy Saving Trust https://energysavingtrust.org.uk/

What is net zero https://netzeroclimate.org/

Project Drawdown www.drawdown.org/

Beyond sustainability, UN Development Programme www.undp.org/

P24 Bianca Pitt, She Changes Climate www.shechangesclimate.org/

P25 Women's Empowerment Principles, UN Global Compact

https://unglobalcompact.org

P31   5 steps to setting powerful intentions, Deepak Chopra

https://chopra.com

Powerful guide to setting intentions, Minimalism made simple

www.minimalismmadesimple.com

BLOG: How to set daily intentions, wholesome culture

https://blog.wholesomeculture.com/how-to-set-daily-intentions/

P35   Start with Why, Simon Sinek

https://simonsinek.com/books/start-with-why/

P38   Ikigai https://ikigai-living.com/

P40   Creative Visualisation, Shakti Gawain

www.amazon.co.uk/Creative-VisualizationShakti-Gawain/dp/1577312295

What is creative visualisation? Better Help

www.betterhelp.com/

P41   The Radical Imagination: Social Movement Research in the
        Age of Austerity, Zedbooks

https://radicalimagination.org/book/

It's not just you, Tori Tsui https://www.toritsui.com/book

What is to What If, Rob Hopkins

www.robhopkins.net/the-book/

Radical Imagination www.everydayactivismnetwork.org/

P47   Lisa Bean https://lisa-bean.com/

P49   Your Best Year Yet! Jinny Ditzler www.waterstones.com/

Dare to Lead, Brené Brown https://brenebrown.com/

P50   Think Globally, Act Locally, Wikipedia

https://en.wikipedia.org/wiki/Think_globally,_act_locally

Atmospheric CO2 www.co2.earth/

P51   Sustainable Development Goals, UNDP

www.undp.org/sustainable-development-goals

P53   Inner Development Goals www.innerdevelopmentgoals.org/

What skills do you need for a sustainable career, Future Learn www.futurelearn.com

P61   Feminine Power, Claire Zammit

https://femininepower.com/

P63   Alchemy for the Mind: Create Your Confident Core: https://www.amazon.co.uk/Alchemy-Mind-Create-Your-Confident/dp/1910056065/

P70   Climate Anxiety Google search trends, Grist

https://grist.org

Young people say climate anxiety is affecting their daily life, CNBC www.cnbc.com

Caroline Hickman, University of Bath Climate Psychology Alliance https://www.climatepsychologyalliance.org/

P71   Katie Hodgetts, The Resilience Project

www.theresilienceproject.org.uk/

P72   How one activist turned eco-anxiety into a force for change, i-news (August 2021) https://inews.co.uk

Clover Hogan, Force of Nature www.forceofnature.xyz/

P73   How to calm your anxiety, Wendy Suzuki, Ted Talks

www.ted.com/talks/

Collective action could relieve climate anxiety, Verywell Mind www.verywellmind.com

Climate change anxiety and mental health, Springer Link https://link.springer.com/

P76   9 therapist approved tips for reframing your existential anxiety, Anna Borges, Self www.self.com/

Feminine Power Academy, Claire Zammit https://femininepower.com/

P77   The power of believing that you can improve, Dr Carol S. Dweck, Ted Talks www.ted.com/talks

Growth mindset: an entrepreneur's best friend, BBC Bitesize

www.bbc.co.uk/bitesize

Reframe your story, Tammy Heerman

www.tammyheermann.com/

P78   9 therapist approved tips for reframing your existential anxiety, Anna Borges, Self

www.self.com/

P81   Canny Conversations, Elaine Warwicker

www.cannyconversations.com/

P86   Climate Solutions at Work, Project Drawdown

www.drawdown.org

What are green jobs and why are they so important, Big Issue

www.bigissue.com

What is net positive? Forum for the Future

www.forumforthefuture.org/

Green jobs, Office for National Statistics (ONS)

www.ons.gov.uk/

P87   Frequently Asked Questions on green jobs (ilo.org)

www.ilo.org

Green Taskforce Report, UK government

www.gov.uk/government/publications/green-jobs-taskforce-report

P89   Green Jobs in UK reach record high in 2021, edie.net

www.edie.net

Global Green Skills Report 2022, LinkedIn

https://news.linkedin.com/2022/february/our-2022-global-green-skills-report

P92   Doughnut Economics, Kate Raworth

www.kateraworth.com/

Green Jobs Taskforce Report, UK government

www.gov.uk/government/publications/green-jobs-taskforce-report

The Green Gap is Expanding, Silicon Canals
https://siliconcanals.com
What are green jobs and why are they important, The Guardian www.theguardian.com/
Green jobs, The Institute for Public Policy Research (IPPR) www.ippr.org

P93   What are green skills? UNIDO www.unido.org
Frequently Asked Questions on green jobs (ilo.org) www.ilo.org
Research into "green jobs", Office of National Statistics www.ons.gov.uk
Rhian Sherrington, Women in Sustainability https://womeninsustainability.net/

P94   How to get a career in sustainability, Silicon Canals https://siliconcanals.com
Upskill for the green jobs of the future, Greenbiz www.greenbiz.com

P95   The Future of Jobs Report 2020, World Economic Forum www.weforum.org
GEO 6 for Youth, UNEP www.unep.org/resources/geo-6-youth

P96   Global Green Skills Report 2022, LinkedIn https://economicgraph.linkedin.com/
What are green skills? UNIDO www.unido.org/stories/what-are-green-skills

P97   Fastest growing green jobs, LinkedIn News www.LinkedIn.com/news/story/the-fastest-growing-green-jobs-5083988/

P100   What does a head of corporate responsibility do? Kirsty Green-Man, Catalyse Change https://catalysechange.com/2023/03/what-does-a-head-of-corporate-responsibility-do/

P101   My sustainability career journey, Vibhati Bhatia, Catalyse Change
https://catalysechange.com/2023/03/my-sustainability-career-journey/

P102   EAUC Sustainability Careers Guide
www.eauc.org.uk/sustainability_careers_guide

P107   Green Education guide, Catalyse Change
https://catalysechange.com/portfolio-item/catalyst-programme-events-outreach/

What is an associate degree, Indeed
https://uk.indeed.com/career-advice

National Careers Service
https://nationalcareers.service.gov.uk/

P110   BLOG: How to find a sustainability internship, Maddy Diment, Catalyse Change
https://catalysechange.com/2022/02/how-to-find-a-sustainability-internship/

P114   BLOG: COP27 Update: 70 Green Apprenticeships, IfATE
https://apprenticeships.blog.gov.uk

BLOG: Six green apprenticeships and how to apply, The Education Hub, gov.uk https://educationhub.blog.gov.uk

P115   What is a green job? - everything you need to know, The Education Hub, gov.uk https://educationhub.blog.gov.uk
Sustainability framework, IfATE
www.instituteforapprenticeships.org

P116   Explore your education and training choices, apprenticeships, National Careers Service
https://nationalcareers.service.gov.uk/

P119   The Solutionists, SolitaireTownsend

https://www.waterstones.com/book/the-solutionists/solitaire-townsend/9781398609327

Q&A Solitaire Townsend, IEMA www.iema.net/articles

P121   The Myers-Briggs type indicator, Verywell mind

www.verywellmind.com/

P122   Truity www.truity.com/

Ce-me colour profiling https://www.colour-profiling.com/

P123   Sustainable Development Goals, UNDP

www.undp.org/sustainable-development-goals

P126   Questions to use during mentoring conversations, The education hub https://theeducationhub.org.nz/

What Is the GROW Coaching Model? Positive Psychology https://positivepsychology.com/

What are the benefits of using the GROW model for coaching, LinkedIn www.LinkedIn.com/

P129   The 7 second CV: How to Land the Interview, James Reed

https://www.amazon.co.uk/Second-CV-How-Land-Interview/dp/0753553074/

Personal statement dos and don'ts, Reed

www.reed.co.uk/career-advice

P134   How to use the STAR technique in interviews, Indeed

https://uk.indeed.com/career-advice/interviewing/star-technique

P135   Ways to follow-up after a job interview, HBR

https://hbr.org

Top 10 Interview Questions, National Careers Service (NCS)

https://nationalcareers.service.gov.uk/careers-advice/top-10-interview-questions

Questions to Ask at an Interview, Indeed

https://uk.indeed.com/career-advice/interviewing/questions-to-ask-at-interview

P139   Why Robots Won't Steal Your Job, Harvard Business Review (HBR) https://hbr.org/

P140   Develop your Soft Skills, NCS https://nationalcareers.service.gov.uk/

The Future of Jobs report 2023, World Economic Forum (WEF) www.weforum.org/

Our 2022 Global Green Skills report, LinkedIn https://news.linkedin.com/2022/february/our-2022-global-green-skills-report

P142   Improve Soft Skills, wikihow.com www.wikihow.com/Improve-Soft-Skills

How to Build a Career in Sustainability, HBR https://hbr.org/

P147-154 LinkedIn Guide, Sabrina Lee https://theimpactagency.org/

P169   Catalyse Change Advisory Board https://catalysechange.com/our-advisory-board/

P170   Tribes, Seth Godin www.sethgodin.com/

P175   Catalyse Change Mentoring Programme, Catalyse Change CIC https://catalysechange.com/portfolioitem/catalyst-summit/

Could you mentor a young woman? Catalyse Change CIC https://catalysechange.com/2021/04/could-you-mentor-a-young-woman/

P181   Fridays for Future https://fridaysforfuture.org/

P182   It's Not That Radical: Climate Action to Transform Our World: https://www.amazon.co.uk/Its-Not-That-Radical-Transform-ebook/dp/B0BT99LG6B/

Girls Resist!: A Guide to Activism, Leadership, and Starting a Revolution:
https://www.amazon.co.uk/Girls-Resist-Activism-Leadership-Revolution/dp/1683690591

P183   What is Intersectionality? The British Academy

www.thebritishacademy.ac.uk/

P184   UK protest rights, National Legal Service

https://nationallegalservice.co.uk/uk-protest-rights/

P187   How to turn climate anxiety into action, Renee Lertzman,

TED Talk www.ted.com/talks

P190   Carbon footprint, Wikipedia

https://en.wikipedia.org/wiki/Carbon_footprint

P196   Jessica Ferrow, Twelve Futures https://twelvefutures.com/

P199   Feminine Power Academy, Clare Zammit

https://femininepower.com/

P200   Your Best Year Yet! Jinny Ditzler

https://www.waterstones.com/book/your-best-year-yet/jinny-ditzler/9780007223220

P201   Megan Fraser, Climate Change coach

https://climatechangecoaches.com/

P205   Imposter syndrome, Cambridge dictionary

https://dictionary.cambridge.org/dictionary/english/impostor-syndrome

Imposter syndrome: you're not alone, Carpenter Smith

business coach www.carpentersmith.com

P207   What is imposter syndrome and how can you combat it?

Elizabeth Cox, Ted Talks www.ted.com/talks

Acknowledgements

To gorgeous SRG, thank you for loving and believing in me. You are so worth the wait.

To darling Kira, I love you to the moon and back. What a wonderful daughter you are.

Big hugs to my mum and sister, too. Thanks for all your love and support.

My dad who is gone but not forgotten; his wisdom and energy still inspire me.

So grateful also to my wonderful friends for all the love, laughter, and adventures.

Huge thanks to:

My brilliant coach Rhian Sherrington, I can't imagine completing this book without your support.

Zoe Montgomery, Kira Gardner, Flo Gregory, Megan Stillwell for your invaluable suggestions.

Nicky Marshall and the Discover Your Bounce Publishing team for making it happen.

My fabulous Catalyse Change fellow Board members: Helen Taylor and Julie Ellison. Along with all our wonderful Advisory Board members, who supported us from the outset: Kate Bruintjes, Sara Telahoun, Jen Best, Heloise Balme, Gemma Perkins, Jessica Ferrow, Rhian Sherrington and Amelia Twine.

Also, to our new Advisory Board members: Darcy Roehling, Emily Goestch, Megan Stillwell, Siobhan Morrin, Sussy Wanjala, Tribeni Chougule, and Vibhatia Bhatia.

Special thanks also go to Jenna Holliday, one of the original co-founders of Catalyse Change, who has been integral to our programme and success.

Catalyse Change sponsors, funders, and partners – thanks for believing in us and making it all possible. They include ERM Foundation, Natracare, Burges-Salmon, Riverford, Vattenfall UK, Pukka Herbs UK, Green Unlimited, Schumacher Institute, Freeths, Bidfood, The National Lottery Community Fund, Bristol City Council, Bristol University, Bristol Green Capital Partnership, Quartet Foundation, Triodos Bank, Wholegrain Digital, UWE, and Women in Sustainability.

Special thanks are due to some of the people from these organisations who have helped us along the way. They include: Amy Robinson, Caroline Vail,

Becky Egan, Kate Bruintjes, Kirsty Green-Mann, Rob Haward, Rufus Ford, Susie Hewson, Vicky Murray, Georgia Phillips, Ian Roderick, and Julie Owst.

Thank you to all the fantastic Catalyse Change speakers, facilitators and mentors who support our catalysts. You do excellent work and make it all possible. Thank you.

So many amazing people and organisations have helped me and Catalyse Change along the way. So even though I can't mention everyone here, please know that I value everyone's support who has made our incredible journey possible. Thank you.

About the author

Traci lives with her partner on a houseboat between Bristol and Bath in southwest England.

They love the herons and kingfishers on the river and exploring it by canoe.

Growing up in a leafy Warwickshire village is where Traci first discovered her love of nature.

However, while travelling in Australia, NZ, and SE Asia during the early 1990s, she witnessed first-hand the destruction of the environment and resulting social inequalities.

On returning to the UK, she discovered Bristol, where she began an 18-year career with the Soil Association. She worked with organic farmers, food producers, and communities around southwest England.

While raising her daughter Kira she became aware of the pressures facing young women, both here and around the world.

This inspired her to set up Catalyse Change CIC in 2016 to help empower girls and young women.

Their innovative sustainability empowerment and green careers programme inspires and upskills young women and non-binary changemakers.

You can connect with Traci and Catalyse Change here:

www.catalysechange.com

www.instagram.com/catalysechange/

www.tracilewis.co.uk

www.LinkedIn.com/in/tracilewis1

www.instagram.com/traci_lewis79

Printed in Great Britain
by Amazon